Salvation, Angels, Giants
and Judgment

The Book of Jude

THE VOICE OF
EVANGELISM

Evangelist
David W. Lankford

ISBN: 978-0-9896525-6-8

If you are unable to obtain a copy of
Salvation, Angels, Giants and Judgment - The Book of Jude
from your local bookstore or library, please write or call:
Evangelist David Lankford
The Voice of Evangelism
P.O. Box 669
Alexis, NC 28006
Phone: 704-263-1945

Printed in the United States of America.

Contents

Introduction

The author of this epistle is known as *"Jude the servant of our Lord Jesus Christ and the brother of James"*. Jude is one of the half-brothers of Christ our Lord. There is very little known concerning the circumstances of those to whom Jude is addressing this letter. Most theologians believe that Jude wrote after Peter's death, but at some point before the destruction of Jerusalem in 70 A.D. The significant similarities between Jude's letter and those of Peter the apostle literally beg for an explanation. The harmony between their epistles is as cohesive as the parallels of the synoptic gospels. It is not a mere coincidence that Jude and Peter are both disturbed by the vast number of false teachers who are so readily accepted by and allowed into the churches. Such apostasy, also addressed by Paul the apostle, seems to have become prevalent throughout the entire church world of that day. It is understandable that Jude would urge believers to 'earnestly contend for the faith, which was once delivered unto the saints.'

Satan did not waste time in his attempt to corrupt the early church with false doctrine and teachers. It is our desire to do an exposition and give a thorough examination, an interpretation to this very short book, deemed by some as the vestibule or antechamber to the book of Revelation. Considering the short length of this epistle, Jude covers an astounding amount of Bible material, evidencing a breadth of extraordinary knowledge, almost more than one could possibly fathom. He takes us from the fall of Lucifer, along with the angels that rebelled with him, to the second coming of Jesus Christ. In twenty-five short verses, Jude gives us more details in short order, than some books of the Bible, which contain a hundred-plus chapters. No mortal man could ever write such a short letter with such immense prophetic insight but by the unction and leadership of the Holy Ghost. Jude was compelled, inspired by the Spirit.

Considering the short length of this epistle, Jude covers an astounding amount of Bible material, evidencing a breadth of extraordinary knowledge, almost more than one could possibly fathom.

I also find the division of the material into twenty-five verses amazing. The first three verses encourage the body of Christ. However, the remaining 22 are profound to say the least. In biblical numerology, the number 22 means light. The candlestick in the holy place had 22 bowls serving the seven lamps. The purpose of the candlestick was to give light. Therefore, Jesus said in Matthew 5:15-16,

> *Neither do men light a candle, and put it under a bushel, but on a candlestick; and it giveth light unto all that are in the house. Let your light so shine before men, that they may see your good works, and glorify your father which is in heaven.*

Jude is attempting to illuminate the hearts and minds of

the early church believers because of the inundation of false prophecies, prophets, teachers, and fallen angels. John himself understood the power of the light for we find his words in John 1:4-5 *"In him was life; and the life was the light of men. And the light shineth in the darkness; and the darkness comprehended it not."*

The darkness cannot admit nor receive the light. I trust that you will always keep the oil in your lamps replenished and your lamp burning brightly. One of the purposes of the Holy Ghost is to keep you full of the oil of God's Spirit. The lamp must be replenished with oil or your light will go out. Because Eli had become indifferent, and his eyes were waxing dim, the lamp of God went out in the tabernacle of God. What a grave tragedy, for the high priest to be in such a personal state that he was not aware the lampstand was no longer burning. Remember, the lampstand was serviced twice a day. The priest would extinguish five of the candles to replenish them with oil and wicks. Once they were re-lighted, he would then extinguish the remaining two and replenish them, as well.

As children of God, we must keep the oil of the Holy Ghost replenished within our earthen vessels. The five wise virgins took oil in their vessels with their lamps. Never before has there been a greater need to keep our lamps trimmed and burning. Thus we read in 1st John 1:7, *"But if we walk in the light, as he is in the light, we have fellowship one with another, and the blood of Jesus Christ his Son cleanseth us from all sin."* The only way anyone can walk in the light is to walk with Christ our Lord.

Jude begins this letter by trying to encourage the early church, but suddenly led by the Holy Ghost, he begins to utter dire warnings concerning heresy and apostasy. He concludes the epistle in an apocalyptic mode. This short book of Jude holds a plethora of knowledge and insight. I trust that you will continue to grow in the grace and the knowledge of our Lord Jesus. It is my desire that you will glean as well as learn untold knowledge from the words of one of the most powerful epistles ever penned by mortal man. Again, this short epistle is like no other in the entirety of the New Testament. We will take each verse and do a brief exegesis. I trust that your knowledge and discernment will explode as you research this profusely short epistle.

Jude 1

Jude, the servant of Jesus Christ, the brother of James, to them that are sanctified by God the father, and preserved in Jesus Christ, and called. (v. 1)

Jude clearly signifies that all believers are sanctified by God the father and are preserved and kept by the power of God through Christ Jesus our Lord. There is a plethora of similarities in Jude's epistle and those of Peter the apostle.

Peter, an apostle of our Lord Jesus Christ, describes how we are preserved as well as kept by the power of God. Notice 1st Peter 1: 5, *"Who are kept by the power of God through faith unto salvation ready to be revealed in the last time"*. Every true believer is called and chosen by God. Peter declared in 2nd Peter 1:10, *"Wherefore the rather, brethren, give diligence to make your calling and election sure: for if you do these things, you shall never fall."* Every child of God can be certain that if they make their calling and election sure they will never fall from the grace of our Lord. We are what we are by the grace of God. Those were Paul's exact words in 1st Corinthians 15:10, *"But by the grace of God I am what I am: and his grace which was bestowed upon me was not in vain."* Certainly, we can do nothing without him, and we should never assume anything different. To do so is unmitigated self-righteousness.

To be sanctified, simply means 'to be set apart' especially for his service, and we have been set apart by the word of God. The church of the living God will remain sanctified or set apart until Christ returns. When Christ returns each believer will receive a glorified body. I know, in the modern church, the doctrine of sanctification is a teaching that has become lost. However, Paul, the apostle, declared in 1st Thessalonians 4:3, *"For this is the will of God, even your sanctification."* I am tremendously saddened and sorrowful as I witness some of the fundamental teachings once taught in the early church that have been completely dismissed in these last days. With modern theology and a loss of perpetuating the true doctrines of Christ, we ultimately fall into heresy and lose our heritage.

> We must never forget that we are the vessels of God wherein God pours his Holy Spirit.

We need more men like Naboth who will not sell or exchange their inheritance for money or popularity. We witness Naboth's Holy Ghost conviction and unyielding disposition as he stood fast against king Ahab found in 1st Kings 21:1-3,

> *And it came to pass after these things, that Naboth the Jezreelite had a vineyard, which was in Jezreel, hard by (beside) the palace of Ahab king of Samaria. And Ahab spake unto Naboth, saying, give me thy vineyard, that I may have it for a garden of herbs, because it is near unto my house: and I will give thee for it a better vineyard than it; or, if it seem good to thee, I will give thee the worth of it in money. And Naboth said to Ahab, the Lord forbid it me, that I should give the inheritance of my fathers unto thee.*

Regretfully, few men still possess that measure of Holy Ghost conviction today. Holy Ghost conviction deters men from doing ungodly things. Once the convicting presence of the Holy Ghost is diminished within the church, men will allow and tolerate ungodly elements to prevail unchecked. Thus, Paul declared in Hebrews 2:1, *"Therefore we are to give the more earnest heed to the things which we have heard, lest at any time we should let them slip."*

The modern church has allowed spiritual and doctrinal truths to slip away. The word *slip* here in the Greek simply means *to run out of like a leaking vessel.* We must never forget that we are the vessels of God wherein God pours his Holy Spirit. I am reminded of Paul's words found here in 2nd Corinthians 4:7, *"But we have this treasure in earthen vessels, that the excellency of the power maybe of God, and not of us."* You see, God has poured the oil of the Holy Spirit within our vessels; thus the power is of God and not of yourselves.

Nevertheless, just like oil or doctrinal teachings man has the proclivity and propensity to let them leak out or slip away. We must stop allowing biblical truths and doctrine to be removed and lost. Any way you interpret it; we are losing spiritual ground.

Jude 2

Mercy unto you, and peace, and love, be multiplied (v. 2).

Jude is admonishing the people of God that the very mercy, peace, and love of God can be multiplied as well as magnified in a believer's life. Needless to say, if the Lord did not magnify those three virtues within the life of every believer, none of us would be here today. The psalmist declared, *"He hath not dealt with us after our sins; nor rewarded us according to our iniquities"* (Psalms 103:10). What would happen to each of us if the Lord rewarded us according to our iniquities and our sins? When I think about the grace of God and how I am afforded the opportunity to allow his love and grace to be magnified within me, it humbles me profusely. Just to know that he would love me in spite of my sins and transgressions baffles me. If a man really understood how unworthy he truly was, he would certainly be more contrite as well as humble. Our pride has blinded us and so we purport foolish measures of pride often times unknowingly! His mercy is truly unfathomable!

We must never forget where we were and what we were when the Holy Ghost drew us to the Father through his Son.

Even though men are born again as new creatures, God does not take away our past memories. To me, my memories are a perpetual reminder of what I was before Christ came into my life. That does not mean that one does not forgive themself of their sins, thus releasing them from their past. Since Christ has forgiven us then we must forgive ourselves. Far too many people live in the past and not in the present.

Some years ago, the Lord gave me a personal word. He said: "Forget the past, embrace the present, and I will take care of your future". I have determined since then to embrace that word with all my heart! When I kneel in prayer and sense his holy presence, I weep in just knowing he has shown me abundant mercy. I am made aware of how unworthy I am of his grace and mercy!

We also read in Psalms 103:17, *"But the mercy of the Lord is from everlasting to everlasting upon them that fear him"*. I trust that each of us will possess the only true and godly fear that will keep men confined to the path of righteousness. If it were not for the mercy of God, many of us would have fallen from the path of righteousness. The psalmist fully understood how terrible sin was, in that it could eviscerate one's life, and one could end on the trash heap of iniquity. Undoubtedly, the psalmist also had a great understanding of the mercy of God, for we read here in Psalms 130:3-4, *"If thou, Lord, shouldest mark iniquities O Lord, who shall stand? But there is forgiveness with thee, that thou mayest be feared."*

If God the father stood before a chalkboard and placed a

mark on it every time, we missed the mark; who could stand? Solomon said; even the thought of foolishness is a sin. Who in this world has never had a foolish idea like being exceedingly rich, tremendously handsome, or exceedingly beautiful? Those are foolish thoughts to say the least. May we all rejoice in the mercy, grace, and redemption that the Lord has shown to each.

If we remain steadfast, I am confident that he will continue to show us the same mercy in the days to come.

Jude 3

Beloved, when I gave all diligence to write unto you of the common salvation, it was needful for me to write unto you, and exhort you that ye should earnestly contend for the faith which was once delivered unto the saints (v. 3).

Jude says that he painstakingly gave all diligence as he sought to write this epistle because he understood the magnitude of its needfulness. This letter was needful because early heresies and fallacious teachings were already trying to pervade and permeate the body of the Lord Jesus Christ.

The term *diligence* in the Greek simply means that Jude had to move with haste and speed lest Satan should usurp what ground the church had already gained. Jude was constrained by the Spirit, distressed by the degree of compromise, and divinely charged with necessity to act quickly. This was a common salvation because it was for both Jews and Gentiles alike. The sacred blood that redeems a Gentile is the same blood that redeems a Jewish person. There is no other offering for the Jews, no matter what some false prophecy teachers advocate and appropriate. Jesus was the only Savior that hung on the cross; thus, there is only one way for the redemption of man.

That is the very purpose of his coming declared by Jesus in John 14:6, *"I am the way, the truth, and the life: no man cometh unto the Father, but by me."* When Jesus said no man, he was simply saying that neither Jew nor Gentile can get to the Father except they come by the way of the cross. That is why Jesus is the only way; there is no another way.

Jude said that we must earnestly *contend* for the faith. To contend simply means to fight for something. Sometimes we struggle in our fight for the faith, and if necessary, we must agonize to keep the faith. Undoubtedly, it will be worth it all in the end. This is truly 'a good fight.' Jude was desirous that we maintain the original faith of the gospel already under assault by false teachers. There seem to be only a few believers today who are agonizing and striving to contend for the true faith. The old cliché is true, "If you can take it, you can make it." It will take much determination, along with spiritual discipline, to endure the hardships that are to come upon the earth here in the time of the end.

Satan will use many things to distract and discourage the child of God, but we must remain faithful through it all. Jesus himself declared in Matthew 24:13, *"But he that shall endure unto the end, the same shall be saved".* The race, my friend, is one of endurance. The church has now entered in to the prophetic times of pain and sorrow. The children of God will have to endure some hardships and trials that may very well be unpleasant and distasteful. David said he had 'never seen the righteous forsaken nor his seed begging bread.' Our strength is in none other than Christ our Lord. Paul, the apostle, declared in Ephesians 6:10. *"Finally, my brethren be strong in the Lord and in the power of his might".*

One cannot possess enough strength to endure on our own. No matter how great your faith, your prayer life, and your knowledge of the scriptures, Satan desires to pierce and riddle our soul to no end. When Jesus told Peter that Satan desired to have his soul, one translation explains that verse this way, *"Peter, Satan has exceedingly demanded that I give him your soul, but I have prayed for thee that your faith will not fail".*

If we keep our faith in Christ alone then we will be able to endure unto the end. That is why we embrace the words of Paul the apostle found in 2nd Timothy 4:16-17, *"At my first answer no man stood with me, but all men forsook me: I pray God that it may not be laid to their charge. Notwithstanding the Lord stood with me and strengthened me."* Paul even said that all men eventually forsook him at the end of his ministry. However, Christ was a present help during the entirety of his troubles.

When the children of God are facing times of loneliness and despair, Jesus Christ will forever remain a present help in the time of trouble. May we all run the race and finish the course, which the Lord has chosen as well as set before us. We must contend to keep the faith to finish our course. This is a good fight and one that we must endure. Paul encouraged his son in the Lord in 1st Timothy 6:12, *"Fight the good fight of faith, lay hold on eternal life, where unto thou art also called, and hast professed a good profession before many witnesses."* The fight that we are fighting is a good fight,

> When the children of God are facing times of loneliness and despair, Jesus Christ will forever remain a present help in the time of trouble.

for it is a fight to seize eternal life.

It is imperative that we maintain our profession of faith before all men in these end times. People today will fight over anything, but they seemingly do not care to fight for the prize of eternal life. May you contend and fight the good fight of faith. The grace of God is sufficient for anyone who desires to contend. One of my favorite passages of Scripture is Acts 20:22-24,

> *And now, behold, I go bound in the spirit unto Jerusalem, not knowing the things that shall befall me there: save that the Holy Ghost witnesseth in every city, saying that bonds and afflictions abide me (are awaiting me). But none of these things move me, neither count I my life dear unto myself, so that I might finish my course with joy, and the ministry, which I have received of the Lord Jesus, to testify the gospel of the grace of God.*

The Holy Ghost was very plainspoken to Paul, the apostle. The Holy Ghost told Paul, in no short order that, in every city, there would be bonds and afflictions awaiting him. Nevertheless, Paul declared emphatically, 'None of these things move me.' Neither did he count his life dear unto himself. The reason Paul did not count his life dear unto himself was so that he might finish the course with joy along with the ministry, which he had received of the Lord Jesus Christ.

If you knew at every turn there was opposition awaiting you, would you remain faithful? Paul did so willingly and so must you!

Jude 4

For there are certain men crept in unawares, who were be-fore of old ordained to this condemnation, ungodly men, turning the grace of our God into lasciviousness, and deny-ing the only Lord God and our Lord Jesus Christ.

In this verse, Jude forewarns the early church that cer-tain men, whose judgment was written about long ago, have stealthily slipped in alongside the believers.

The Greek word *crept* means to *lodge stealthily.* These god-less men have changed the grace of our Lord Jesus Christ into a license to sin. These men would deny Jesus Christ, our only sovereign Lord and Savior. They would seek to find a place of residence within the church of the living God, without our knowing them as ungodly. Jesus himself forewarned of these imposters who would come in the strength of his name. Jesus declared here in Matthew 24:5, *"For many shall come in my name, saying, I am Christ; and shall deceive many".*

Many today, in the nominal church world, use the power of Christ's name to take advantage of weak and anemic Chris-tians. They are subtle in their presentation and duplicitous. They behold the sheep of God through their eyes as a wolf. Jesus also declared in Matthew 7:15-16, *"Beware of false prophets which come to you in sheep's clothing, but inwardly they are ravening wolves. Ye shall know them by their fruits."* These pretenders are religious, and they feign the Spirit of Christ through their outward cloaks of self-righteousness. On the inside, they are nothing more than ravaging wolves. They plunder and pillage the body of the Lord Jesus Christ for their own personal gain.

Paul, the apostle, gave us a dire warning in how these charlatans would infiltrate the church of the living God. We read in Acts 20:29-31,

> *For I know this that after my departing shall grievous wolves enter in among you, not sparing the flock. Also of our own selves shall men arise, speaking perverse things, to draw away disciples after them. Therefore, watch and remember that, by the space of three years, I ceased not to warn every one night and day with tears.*

False prophets and charlatans never spare the flock, but rather they fleece and devour the flock of God. It would not be long after Paul's departing that these grievous wolves would come into the church and seek their prey. They never protect, care, nurture, or provide for the flock of God; they are totally self-serving.

Paul went on to say that these men would portray themselves to be like him, and feign apostleship *(of our own selves shall men arise).* Paul, having the gift of discernment, knew that these men would speak lies as well as distort the truth of God's holy word. By those means and methods, they would draw unto themselves disciples and cause the people to become followers of them and not Christ.

To demonstrate the voracious appetite of these wolves,

two very prominent prophecy teachers are now teaching that you can take the mark of the beast in the end times and remain saved. They purport this false teaching, because they claim that taking the mark is not the unpardonable sin. That totally contradicts Revelation 20:4.

> *And I saw thrones, and they sat upon them, and judgment was given unto them: and I saw all the souls of them that were beheaded for the witness of Jesus, and for the word of God, and which had not worshipped the beast, neither his image, neither had received his mark upon, their foreheads, or in their hands; and they lived and reigned with Christ a thousand years.*

This verse makes it clear that men must overcome the mark of the beast - both his name and his number, and that they must not worship his image. Once false doctrine begins to grow, it will explode exponentially, now as then.

These men, in Jude's day, were adding and taking away from the word of God. They no longer embraced the validity of God and his word. Here again, Peter, the apostle, confirms the words of Jude in 2nd Peter 3:15-17,

> *And account that the long-suffering of our Lord is salvation; even as our beloved brother Paul also according to the wisdom given unto him hath written unto you; as also in all his epistles, speaking in them of these things; in which are some things hard to be understood, which they that are unlearned and unstable wrest (twist or convolute), as they do also the other scriptures, unto their own destruction.*
>
> *Ye, therefore, beloved, seeing ye know these things before, beware lest ye also, being led astray with the error of the wicked, fall from your own steadfastness.* (KJV)

The cohorts of Satan have always been intent on steering men to twist the Holy Scriptures to their own destruction. This

deception leads these followers to fall from their own stead-
fastness. False prophets create division and confusion within
the church so that the misguided would follow them and not
the Holy Spirit.

Paul declared that over a period of three years, from Mi-
letus to Ephesus, he warned the church untiringly because he
knew the slaughter that Satan would unleash within the early
church. Today there seems to be a disposition of not caring
whether the sheep are either slaughtered or dismembered,
spiritually or emotionally. Paul was not only untiring, but he
wept profusely day and night to give them early warning of
evil men that would seek to seduce them and lead them astray.

The prophet Jeremiah possessed the same spiritual despair
prior to the Babylonian captivity. Note Jeremiah 9:1, *"Oh, that
my head were waters, and mine eyes a fountain of tears, that
I might weep day and night for the slain of the daughter my
people!"* This verse describes a man of God who is concerned
about the flock of God. Jeremiah was concerned about their
physical and spiritual destiny. We know from Jude's letter for
a certainty that Satan sought early on to corrupt the church of
the living God.

How long did it take for Satan, from the newly created
heavens and the earth to seek entrance into the Garden of
Eden so that he might destroy Adam and Eve? I personally
think it was a very short period of time following creation and
the placement of Adam and Eve in the garden. Satan quickly
sought an avenue into the garden. He was determined to dis-
rupt everything that God had planned from the beginning of
the foundations of the world. I believe he untiringly fought
with an unmitigated deception to find his way into the garden.

He, no doubt, approached many of God's creatures and tried to coerce them, so as to possess them. However, all but one of them answered and said, *You will have no place of residence within us.*

Then Satan approached the serpent, which the Bible says was more subtle than any beast of the field. I am confident the serpent did not perceive that Satan would bring him to such a place of utter destruction. The serpent never thought he would be cursed to live perpetually in the dust of the ground. Even though God created every creature from the dust of the earth, he cursed the serpent or bound him to his belly, and dust he would eat all the days of his life. One Hebrew translation reads, regarding the serpent, *You are banned from all other animals and condemned to the soil.*

Adam and Eve never discerned their ultimate demise following their disobedience. All men, seemingly never discern how destructive Satan is and how he will ultimately ruin their lives while deceiving them. Never underestimate the power of Satan as he seeks to coerce you and me down a path of pleasure and illusionary beauty. It is apparent that men never discern the chaos and destruction that Satan wills for their lives. Every proposition that Satan ever made to a man appears harmless and innocent in the beginning. From Adam and Eve to the mighty man Sampson, and even to the sweet psalmist David, they never discerned Satan's desire concerning their destruction.

> Do not ever underestimate the power of Satan as he seeks to coerce you and me down a path of pleasure and illusionary beauty.

Each of us must remain sober and completely understand

that when Satan approaches us, it is with a goal and desire of ultimately destroying us. He will make things look so pleasant, pleasing and beautiful, but recognize that, beneath that veneer, there is nothing but rot, ruin, and spiritual decay. Beneath his reptilian scales, there is nothing more than putrefying sores. He wants to pass that putrefaction into your life. Satan has never done anything good to bless or comfort anyone through his ungodly relationships. He will only bring you death, decay, and ruination. This noxious creature that creeps, hisses, and stings is out for your death. He is truly a cold-blooded treacherous murderer and villain.

All the death and chaos that the world knows and experiences is by the expression of this one spiritual creature. This one spiritual being alone has caused unfathomable damage. But, thank God, there is a judgment day in which all will bow before the King of glory, and that includes Satan. Notice the words of Paul, the apostle, in Galatians 2:4-5,

> And that because of false brethren unawares brought in, who came in privily to spy out our liberty which we have in Christ Jesus, that they might bring us into bondage: To whom we gave place by subjection, no, not for an hour; that the truth of the gospel might continue with you.

Here in this passage, Paul describes the purported believers as false brethren. Though they had become members of the church, they were sinister in their deeds. These false brethren desired to share in the churches fellowship, characterized by life and love, but in reality, they were not so inwardly in character and therefore they had no right to be considered true brethren. They professed brotherhood, but a genuine relationship and fellowship of the Holy Ghost was missing in their lives.

The word *privily* in the Greek means to *'come in stealthily.'* Just like stealth fighter jets in the United States Air Force, these false prophets and charlatans desired to come into the church unnoticed and undetected. Much like these fighter jets, this is all by design and architecture; however, it is a satanic design. The fact that Jude declares these men to be ungodly means they are without fear and reverence of God. They practice and teach the very opposite of what godly fear demands of each of us. Having once been godly, they have now fallen from grace, and they are now ungodly. Paul completely understood those men to be false brethren thus he gave them no place neither subjected himself to them in any way not even for an hour. Paul would not suffer himself to be under their subjection because he knew if he did, then the gospel of the Lord Jesus Christ would not be able to continue. Because they were false brethren, he understood he would never change their minds even though he was the one who had received the revelation of Jesus Christ and the plan of redemption.

Paul made that vividly clear in Galatians 1:11-12, *"But I certify you, brethren, that the gospel which was preached of me is not after man. For I neither received of man neither was I taught it, but by the revelation of Jesus Christ."* The revelation was the way of the cross and not the law. Furthermore, he would never allow false brethren of Satan to deter him from God's service.

I want to emphasize the term "false brethren". These false brethren attempted in a deceptive manner to promote themselves in the eyes of Paul. Their purpose was to hinder, as well as impede the work of God. Paul made it very clear, whatever they were; it made no matter or difference to him, because God accepts no man's personage. Whether in personal meetings or conference, Paul said that these men were unable to add anything to him. Though they apparently tried to consult with him and coerce him, Paul knew they were still false brethren, true pretenders. Let me admonish you as well that these charlatans will add nothing to your life.

Jude went on to say that they also deny the only Lord God. Simply put, these false brethren no longer knew the Lord Jesus Christ, and they denied him in repudiating the very fundamental truths of the word of God. Men do not have to stand openly and deny Christ to be seen for what they are. They deny him by their apostasy and false doctrines. They would never see the error within themselves because they are deceived. That is the problem with deception; men think they are right, but they are absolutely wrong. I trust that you may never be deceived no matter what Satan may wield against you. The term *deceived,* in the Greek, simply means *fraudulence, to err,* along with *being seduced from orthodoxy.*

> I trust that you may we never be deceived no matter what Satan may wield against us.

Paul warned us about how these deceivers would operate found here in 2nd Timothy 3:13, *"But evil men and seducers shall wax worse and worse, deceiving and being deceived"*. In spite of the clarity of God's holy word, they continue to divorce themselves from biblical principles. In retrospect, they gainsay and speak evil contrary to what God has already spoken in his holy word. This is one of the subtle trademarks of false teachers. They do not preach nor teach false doctrine in boxcar letters, but it is all in the fine print. Their speeches are full of deception and duplicity. Whether in subtle differences or nuances, they are the epitome of error. They deny the Lord Jesus Christ and the truthfulness of his holy word.

Satan only added one word to discount God's truth in the Garden. He added the little three-letter word not to the word of God and so he said, "Ye shall *not* surely die." That is how simple and quickly he challenged, as well as distorted, the truthfulness of God's word. You are witnessing the very same things in the modern church era. May we all take heed and be aware of these ungodly charlatans and pretenders. They have entered into many churches and denominations in this stealth mode. However, the word of God and the Holy Ghost will expose these charlatans if we walk in the Holy Ghost. The spirit of truth will always counter the spirit of error.

Notice the words of John in 1st John 4:6, *"We are of God: he that knoweth God heareth us; he that is not of God heareth not us. Hereby know we the spirit of truth, and the spirit of error."* I trust you will always discern the spirit of truth verses the spirit of error.

Jude 5

I will, therefore, put you in remembrance though ye once knew this, how that the Lord, having saved the people out of the land of Egypt, afterward destroyed them that believed not.

Jude, just as the apostle Peter, wanted to bring the people's mind into a place of remembrance. Both men wanted the people of God to aggregate their thoughts concerning the truth. Too often, we forget the things that God has spoken in times past and thus, Jude wants to stir up our minds by way of remembrance. It is easy to forget things God has spoken and revealed to us. For that reason, Jude used the phrase – *'though ye once knew this.'* Obviously, they once knew this fundamental truth, but it had somehow now escaped them.

This is why Paul gave the powerful admonition in Hebrews 2:1, *"Therefore we ought to give the more earnest heed to the things which we have heard, lest at any time we should let them slip."* The term *slip* here in the Greek means to *run out of like a leaking vessel.* We are to never allow the word of God to leak from these clay jars in which we all live.

Jude wants us to remember, how the Lord, having saved

the Israelites out of the land of Egypt, afterward destroyed them because they no longer believed in him. Regretfully, one of the greatest heretical teachings having presently permeated the church of our Lord Jesus Christ is the *"once saved always saved doctrine"*. This particular passage here in Jude refutes that doctrine completely. Jude says that the Lord, having saved

> Do not ever think that you can continue to live in sin and rebellion and retain the blessings of God.

them, would also destroy them. Why would you save something and then destroy it, if it had not been marred beyond the hope of restoration, lost, in a redemptive sense? They were *lost* because they had abandoned their faith in the Lord. Having been delivered from Egypt's bondage, they turned away from the faith that once delivered them.

The Israelites stopped *contending for the faith;* therefore, they *lost* their opportunity for salvation and deliverance, and died in the wilderness. Do not ever think that you can continue to live in sin and rebellion and retain the blessings of God. We read in Hebrews 3:12, *"Take heed, brethren, lest there be in any of you an evil heart of unbelief, in departing from the living God."* Notice the harmony in what Jude said in his epistle and what Paul says in his epistle to the Hebrews. The Holy Ghost always brings clarity and harmony when inspiring the Holy Writ. Paul, the apostle, declared here in Hebrews 3:17, *"But with whom was he grieved 40 years? Was it not with them that had sinned, whose carcasses fell in the wilderness?"* This Scripture passage makes it clear that because of their sin, the Holy Spirit was grieved; thus, they died in the wilderness and were unable to inherit the promise land.

Their failure to inherit the promise land was both literal and spiritual. It will be the same for all who no longer contend for the faith and choose to fall by the wayside. The Israelites never inherited the promise of God and so shall it be with all who backslide and stop contending for the faith. Again, every child must contend for the faith and endure to the end.

Enduring is not always easy, but Jesus said, *'if we would endure unto the end we shall be saved.'* Adam and Eve were the personification of two people who had everything including eternal life and yet they lost it because of sin and disobedience. If it is impossible for men to lose their salvation and with it the blessing of God because of sin, explain to me what happened to them? They were immediately excommunicated from the very presence of God, because of sin and disobedience.

Be careful what you believe!

Jude 6

And the angels which kept not their first estate, but left their own habitation, he hath reserved in everlasting chains under darkness unto the judgment of the great day."

Jude is describing the angels that rebelled along with Lucifer and participated in his ungodly fall. These angels left the principality and domain in which God had placed them from the beginning of creation. They simply abandoned God's plan and purpose for his eternal kingdom. They rebelled and left their habitation or place of residence. These fallen angels not only sought, but they invaded the sphere and realm of humanity. They crossed a divine and forbidden border that God had established from creation. They broke through what I call *spiritual membranes.*

These fallen angels ultimately married human women and took them as wives in order to corrupt the human race. They sought to corrupt the human stock so they could prevent the coming of our Lord Jesus Christ. Think of that idea: they sought to keep the Creator from coming to his creation and redeeming humankind, the race of men, made in his image and in his likeness.

Satan was trying to corrupt the promised seed. We read in Genesis 3:15, *"And I will put enmity between thee and the woman, and between thy seed and her seed; it shall bruise thy head, and thou shalt bruise his heel"*. Some time ago, while I was in prayer, the Lord put a word in my spirit, and that word was interference. Satan has always desired to interpose himself in a way that hinders or impedes the plan of God. We do not understand the gravity of Satan's rebellion and the damage he has committed. He has continued to invoke chaos upon the plan of God and the destruction of humanity.

From this prophetic word given to Eve in the Garden of Eden, Satan sought profusely to corrupt the seed. This corruption was for the express purpose in negating the birth of Jesus Christ. Jesus Christ was the promised seed. May we seek to understand the gravity of the message Jude is conveying. I trust that you can fathom what actually took place before Satan's rebellion, after his rebellion, and in the fall of Adam and Eve in the garden. Satan moved with untold haste after having been thrown out of heaven, to corrupt humankind.

> From this prophetic word given to Eve in the Garden of Eden, Satan sought profusely to corrupt the seed.

Jesus declared in Luke 10:18, *"And he said unto them; I beheld Satan as lightning fall from heaven"*. The word *beheld* in the Greek means *to be a spectator* and *to look with interest for the purpose of careful observation to the details*. We read in Genesis 6:1-4,

> *And it came to pass, when men began to multiply on the face of the earth, and daughters were born unto them, That the sons of God saw the daughters of men that they were fair, and they took them wives of all which they chose. And*

the Lord said, My spirit shall not always strive with man, for that he also is flesh: yet his days shall be hundred and twenty years. There were giants in the earth in those days; and also after that, when the sons of God came in unto the daughters of men, and they bare children to them, the same became mighty men (warriors and giants) which were of old, men of renown.

Here in Genesis, the women were described as being fair, which means, *to be pleasing, desirable, and beautiful.* These fallen angels sought to conceive children through these earthly women. This hybrid creation, through fallen angels and women, was the very origin of Greek mythology, of the giants and the men of renown. We know that these men were literal giants, because we read here in Deuteronomy 3:11,

For only Og King of Bashan remained of the remnant of giants; behold, his bedstead was a bedstead of iron; is it not in Rabbath of the children of Ammon? Nine cubits was the length thereof (18 feet long), and four cubit's the breath of it, (over 8 feet wide) after the cubit of a man.

The progeny of fallen angels with the daughters of Adam are called *Nephilim,* which means *fallen ones.* What we fully know and understand can only come strictly from the word of God. They were evidently great in physical size but also great in their wickedness and iniquities. They were superhuman, abnormal beings, and their destruction was necessary for the preservation of the human race. Great in stature, some of them had six fingers and six toes. Their spears weighed between 10-25 pounds. Some theologians believe the coat of armor that Goliath wore weighed nearly 200 pounds and that he may have been 13 feet tall weighing between 900 and 1200 pounds. For this very reason, the flood came upon the world of the ungodly. God destroyed the corrupted human seed on the earth. The sin of these angels was deemed comparable to the sins of Sodom and Gomorrah. In verse seven of Jude, he uses the phrase *'in like manner'*.

There were possibly two separate acts of rebellion by Lucifer and the fallen angels. The first rebellion would be the one, which caused the end of the world that was. After God cast out Lucifer from the heavens, the cosmos was obliterated, suffering destruction, its created form marred. After the Luciferian fall, we see the re-creation of heaven and earth in Genesis 1:1, where the Scripture says, *'the Spirit of God began to move upon the face of the waters'*. This was undoubtedly, followed by a second rebellion. It is in this rebellion when the sons of God or fallen angels, took unto themselves human wives. Their offspring was giants as we previously stated, known as the *Nephilim,* and they were monsters of iniquity. These giants were superhuman in size and character. The purpose of the flood was to destroy them all.

I may startle some of you now, but Jesus said in Matthew 24:37-39,

> *But as the days of Noah were, so shall also the coming of the Son of man be. For as in the days that were before the flood they were eating and drinking, marrying and giving in marriage, until the day that Noah entered into the ark, And knew not until the flood came, and took them all away; so shall also the coming of the Son of Man be.*

I know people grapple to believe that we could see giants or aliens in these last days. In truth, some television networks are already preparing people for such an event. Not too long ago, there was a TV series known as the "V" involving a colony of reptiles that had come to the earth to purportingly help humanity. In the end, their intent was to destroy the human race and create a reptilian society. Needless to say, that is Satan's objective in this present hour. He wants to set up a new world order so that men can live in sinful perpetuity. But, Jesus said, *"As it was in the days of Noah, so shall it be also in the coming of the Son of Man."*

If you cannot embrace the existence of giants in a previous world, then you might grapple with giants or aliens in the near future. However, I trust you can believe the second scenario about which Jesus spoke concerning the last days. He said in Luke 17:28, *"Likewise also as it was in the days of Lot; they did eat, they drank, they bought, they sold, they planted, they builded."* If you have trouble believing in giants or aliens, start believing in sodomy as the cultural norm! Homosexuality is running rampant throughout the world and especially here in the United States.

In 2012, the United States Supreme Court agreed to embrace same sex marriage and made it legal for those who chose that life style. People of the same sex can now marry legally. Jesus gave us two scenarios concerning end time events. If you cannot believe in both of them, I

> If Satan could accomplish this, then the word of God would fail, and Satan and his doom would be averted.

trust that you can at least consider if not embrace, the one we face today. The Genesis eruption of fallen angels mixing with human women was Satan's first attempt to prevent the promised seed, Jesus Christ, from ever appearing. If Satan could accomplish this, then the word of God would fail, and Satan and his doom would be averted.

As soon as it was known and revealed by God, that the seed of the woman would come through the lineage of Abraham, there was another attempt to destroy the seed, promised by God. That is why we see in Genesis 6:4, *"There were giants in the earth in those days; and also after that"*. It is evident that, after the flood, there was a second attempt by these fallen Angels to pollute the human seed, evidently smaller in number and more limited in scope - for the most part confined to Canaan.

Most Bible scholars believe that the Noachian flood took place 500 years after the fall of Adam and Eve. Satan's aim and desire was to occupy the land of Canaan before Abraham. Again, Satan was attempting to negate the promised seed from ever coming. We read in Genesis 12:6, *"And Abram passed through the land unto the place of Sichem, onto the plain of Moreh. And the Canaanite was then in the land."* The giants *(Canaanites)* were already in the land of Canaan, and they would try to thwart Abraham's efforts because of the covenant that God had made with him concerning the promised seed.

We also know that there were giants after the flood. Israel, following their Exodus from Egypt, would have to contend with these hybrid and wicked creatures known as giants. We read about their dilemma in Numbers 13:33, *"And there we saw the giants, the sons of Anak, which come of the giants: and we were in our own sight as grasshoppers, and so we were in their sight."* Remember, only Caleb and Joshua believed that that they were able to conquer the Canaanites *(giants)* that had already possessed the land. The giants were to be cut off, driven out and utterly destroyed. Israel failed in doing so, and we do not know how many giants got away to other countries to escape the general destruction. If we had more details concerning their escape it might help us to solve many questions connected with scriptural anthropology *(theology dealing with the origin, nature, and destiny of human beings).* Needless to say, these were not true human beings. They were a crossbreed or a hybrid if you please. It is certain that the second eruption took place after the flood but before Genesis 14.

These giants were integrated with five nations, which included Sodom and Gomorrah and were defeated by the four Kings under Chedorlaomer. We know this to be a fact according to Genesis 14:5,

> *And in the fourteenth year came Chedorlaomer, and the King's that were with him, and smote the Rephaims in Asheroth Karnaim, and the Zuzims in Ham, and the Emimis in Shaveh Kiriathaim.*

The Rephaims, Zuzims, and Emims were all giant tribes; that is, they were giants in size but not in number. The untold strength of these giants is witnessed in cities such as Bashan to this day. Many theologians believe they were instrumental in the building and construction of the pyramids in Egypt, which remains an unsolved problem and mystery even in our times. Let us not forget, these giants were renowned or famous, of great report.

Satan never ceased in attempting to corrupt the seed, which would come through Abraham. When Abram journeyed to Egypt, Genesis 12, Pharaoh tried to take Sarai and place her in his harem because she was very fair or beautiful woman. God Almighty intervened to protect the promised seed that was to come through this couple. The Lord plagued Pharaoh and his house with great plagues because of Sarai, Abram's wife. Since the Lord had given this prophecy in Genesis 3:15, he would have to fight untiringly to bring that prophecy to fruition.

We see a second attempt in Genesis 20, as King Abimelech sought to corrupt the promised seed once again by taking Sarah as his own. However, God came to Abimelech in a dream by night and said, *"Behold thou art but a dead man for the woman which thou hast taken she is a man's wife."* God also reminded Abimelech that Abraham was a prophet of God, and that Abraham would pray for him, and he would live. If Abraham did not pray for him and Abimelech did not restore Sarah to him, then he would surely die.

Since the prophecy given in Genesis 3:15, Satan has always tried to prevent the seed from ever coming to fruition. One of Satan's final attempts to stop the seed was through Joseph, the husband of Mary. Satan sought to put fear into Joseph's heart and cause him to abandon the plan of God. We read in Matthew 1:19-20,

> *Then Joseph her husband, being a just man, and unwilling to make her a public example, was minded to put her away privily. But while he thought on these things, behold, the angel of the Lord appeared unto him in a dream, saying, Joseph, thou son of David, fear not to take unto thee Mary thy wife; for that which is conceived in her is of the Holy Ghost.*

The Bible says that Joseph was a *just* man meaning, "He kept the law". It was not truly in his heart to put Mary away. For the biblical rights in putting a woman away, we look to the Torah, Deuteronomy 24:1,

> *When a man hath taken a wife, and married her, and it come to pass that she find no favor in his eyes, because he*

hath found some uncleanness in her: then let him write her
a bill of divorcement, and give it in her hand, and send her
out of his house.

Joseph had no doubt thought to divorce Mary, and that
is why the Lord said to him in a dream, *"Fear not to take unto*
thee Mary thy wife". Finally, Jesus would go the cross, die there,
and his body was then laid in the borrowed sepulcher. A watch
by Roman soldiers was both ordered and then dutifully executed. The stone covering the tomb was sealed. Then, on the
third day, Jesus rose from the dead. I rejoice in the fact that
God Almighty has always out-gunned the devil in any match
up!

For this sin of fornication, the Lord has reserved these
fallen angels in everlasting chains under darkness kept until
the judgment of the great day. We have two classes of angels:
the chained and the unchained. The unchained will obviously
fight with Satan against Michael and his angelic host, which
will be at the very beginning of the great tribulation. Michael,
the Archangel, is the restrainer that is found in 2nd Thessalonians 2:7, *"For the mystery of an iniquity doth already work:*
only he who now letteth will let, until he be taken out of the way."
The 'he' in this passage is not the Holy Ghost, nor the church,
but Michael the Archangel.

Once Michael is taken out of the way, he will ascend up
into the heavens and make war with Satan. We find this truth
in Revelation 12:7, *"And there was war in heaven: Michael and*
his angels fought against the dragon, and the dragon fought and
his angels." When the Lord chained these angels is uncertain
and how long after the flood he chained them is pure specula-
tion and conjecture. Nevertheless, it is sure and scriptural, that

there were giants after the days of the Noachian flood.

Some time ago, the Lord revealed to me that these fallen angels are the ones that have taught men the most powerful perversions that have ever existed. It is not within the natural boundaries and confines of the minds of men to commit the abomination's we now witness today. Sodomy, bestiality, child molestation, along with bizarre rituals and murders, almost beyond description beg for a supra-human explanation - they were taught to men by these fallen angels.

The reason men are capable of these bizarre perversions is because of man's fallen nature. The angels, having already fallen prior to man's fall, passed on their filth, degradation and deprivation to men who had also fallen from their first estate *(Adam)*. These fallen angels had tremendous knowledge, both spiritual and physical. When coupled with Adam's knowledge, it is truly unfathomable, in contrast, the far depths and reach of these corrupted and polluted minds.

Adam was not a formally educated man nor a learned man. When God brought forth Adam from the earth, I believe that he was the equivalent in development of a full-grown man, about 30 years of age. In his creation, God deposited in Adam untold knowledge and wisdom. His vocabulary must have literally been off the charts, having thousands, if not tens-of-thousands of words. We know that from Genesis 2:19,

> *And out of the ground the Lord God formed every beast of the field, and every fowl of the air; and brought them unto Adam to see what he would call them: and whatsoever Adam called every living creature, that was the name thereof.*

If you take Adam's knowledge, after the fall, and couple it with that of the fallen angels and their knowledge, the depths and extensiveness of sin are unfathomable. We as Christians are blessed to have never known the depths of such deprivation and depravity. There are some things better left unknown. We read in Ecclesiastes 1:18, *"For in much wisdom is much grief: and he that increaseth knowledge increaseth sorrow."*

We are never to give place to the devil, and that includes our mind. Thus we are admonished in Ephesians 4:23, *"And be renewed in the spirit of your mind"*. I feel constrained by the Holy Ghost to elaborate no further or dig any deeper on this subject. I am sure you understand why. What a blessing, to walk in the purity of God's holy love. In Jude 6, those particular angels are chained, evidently in everlasting chains under darkness, awaiting the Great White Throne Judgment and Jude describes that as *"the judgment of the great day"*.

Jude 7

Even as Sodom and Gomorrah, and the cities about them in like manner, giving themselves over to fornication, and going after strange flesh, and are set forth for an example, suffering the vengeance of eternal fire.

The sins of Sodom and Gomorrah, like that of the angels found in Genesis 6, are unnatural. Both angels and men broke through the bounds or *spiritual membranes* God had set. Both angels and men, relative to God's creation, both had a free moral choice.

Just because God created angels and men, he does not dictate their choices. Angels and men can do as they please, and that is manifested profusely within the earth from man's perspective. From Jude's epistle, it is also true within the heavenlies, because of the fallen and rebellious angels. We see that the fallen angels took unto themselves wives, which they chose with intent and purpose. Not only did the fallen angels cross the boundaries that God had set for them, it is obvious to me that women also crossed those boundaries.

Women at one point or another gave themselves over to these fallen angels or were seduced by them. Women chose to cross a boundary in giving themselves over to these fallen angels. I believe that it was a decision they made in yielding themselves to these giants. When the scripture indicated that the sons of God chose them as wives, it means that they selected them or that they judged their choice after having tested that option. It was a deliberate and well thought-out decision. Had those women resisted and never crossed the natural limits of God, then giants would have never been born.

No doubt, there was a tremendous temptation, along with a profound spirit of seduction, to coerce these women to cross such a line, a boundary that God had predetermined. As a free moral agent, these women had the right to say, 'No!' and resist the evil, that is, if they had possessed any conscience whatsoever. We are told in Genesis 6:5, "*And God saw that the wickedness of man (and women) was great in the earth, And that every imagination (the whole imagination) of the thoughts of his heart was only evil continually*". Not only were their imaginations evil, but their purposes and desires were also evil. They apparently sought an experience beyond the realm of normalcy, as well. There was an obvious demand by Satan to seduce these women as partners in helping him to destroy the promised seed.

It was the serpent, in the garden; that was instrumental in deceiving the woman and corrupting her. Satan would once again seek out the weaker vessel to further his diabolical plan to try to stop the promised seed. Paul validates this biblical truth in 2nd Corinthians, "*But I fear, lest by any means, as the ser-*

pent beguiled (seduced wholly) Eve through his subtlety (trick-ery, sophistry, and craftiness) so your minds should be corrupted (to be ruined by moral influence) from the simplicity that is in Christ." Satan and the fallen angels evidently seduced and cor-rupted these women and they yielded themselves to indulge in the worse kind of sexual immorality. We are speaking of earthly women cohabiting with celestial beings. The fact that all men were evil in their thoughts confirms that the women were, as well.

Not only did fallen angels desire the women, but the evil women also desired that which was not natural. We find this truth in Genesis 6: 2, *"That the sons of God saw the daughters of men that they were fair; and they took them wives of all which they chose."* The fact that the fallen angels chose these women leads me firmly to believe that there were other women who would not respond to the angelic appeals and aberrant choic-es. Some women refused to follow this road of destruction and utter chaos. However, some did choose to go after strange flesh as Jude describes.

Most Bible scholars believe that these daughters were ac-tually from Adam, not from Noah's three sons or from the line of Cain. After the flood, Noah and his family were the only pure human stock left in the earth without having been corrupted in some way by the fallen angels. Satan was trying to infiltrate every aspect of humanity to destroy the promised seed. We have no true Bible knowledge as to how many angels in number actually rebelled with Lucifer, but according to the book of Revelation, we believe that he drew one third of the angelic host. We read in Revelation 12:3-4,

And there appeared another wonder in heaven; and behold

a great red dragon (Lucifer) having seven heads (the seven Dispensational satanic kingdoms) and ten horns, and seven crowns upon his heads. And his tail drew the third part of the stars of heaven, and did cast them to the earth: and the dragon stood before the woman (Israel, Gen.37:9 pertains to Joseph's dream) which was ready to be delivered, for to devour her child as soon as it was born.

This Scripture tells us that Satan drew one third of the *stars* by his tail. The term *drew* in Greek means *to drag or to hale.* When Satan fell, he drew one third of the angels along with him. We also have a scripture confirming that Satan was cast out of heaven and that other angels, we believe a third, rebelled and fell with him. That scripture is Revelation 12:9, *"And the great dragon was cast out, that old serpent, called the Devil, and Satan, which deceiveth the whole world: he was cast out into the earth, and his angels were cast out with him."*

Now we see that he drew a third part of the stars or angels from heaven, and they were cast out with him. This Scripture also tells us that, through his open rebellion, there was worldwide deception, which leads us to believe; that is why Noah was the only pure stock left in the earth. Lucifer was able to deceive the whole world, but Noah had found grace in the eyes of God. Just like men, angels are also called the sons of God, because He created them, as well. We know this from Job 1:6-7,

Now there was a day when the sons of God came to present themselves before the Lord, and Satan came also among them. And the Lord said unto Satan, Whence comest thou? Then Satan answered the Lord, and said, From going to and fro in the Earth, and from walking up and down in it.

Jude declares, not only did the cities of Sodom and Gomorrah go after strange flesh, but also the cities about them or in close proximity did the same. The word *fornication* in Greek is *porneno* (Strong's: # 1608), and it means to be *utterly unchaste* or *bawdy*. The fallen angels went after strange flesh, thus crossing the bounds that God had set within his creation.

I personally believe, following the fall of these rebellious angels, they begin to sodomize one another. We know that angels are not sexless, because they were able to procreate through women. All angels are male, and there are no records of their ever being female angels. The fact that the Bible never discloses or shares with us that there are female angels is why I believe they sodomized one other. These angels suddenly looked upon the daughters of men, saw that they were beautiful, and desired them for wives. These angels now served Lucifer, and thus he put it in their hearts to fulfill his lust. It is a fact, 'No man can serve two masters.' These fallen angels faithfully served Lucifer, the devil. Satan instrumentally put it in their hearts to attempt to corrupt the promised seed from coming. Satan, the father of these fallen angels, now sought to fulfill his lust.

Jesus gives us a measure of insight when he spoke these words in John 8:44,

> *Ye are of your father the devil, and the lust of your father ye will do. He was a murderer from the beginning, and abode not in the truth, because there is no truth in him. When he speaketh a lie, he speaketh of his own: for he is a liar, and the father of it.*

These fallen angels acted out the lust of their father, the devil, in order to corrupt the promised seed. This is where the giants came from. This was Satan's plan, commanding the fallen angels to procreate with the daughters of men. The giants were the offspring and by-product of fallen angel's liaisons with earthly women. God did not breathe into the nostrils of angels, so they do not have a soul, but they certainly possess a spirit. I believe, when these giants died physically, their remains returned to the earth, just as those of humans, but their disembodied spirit are now the demons that run rampant throughout the earth. Just like this present administration in the White House said, *"Never let a good crisis go to waste".* Satan is frugal, spiritually, in using the spirit of the giants to continue to try to corrupt the plan of God. From my biblical studies, I find no origin of demons whatsoever in the Holy Scriptures. These giants no doubt have a spirit, but there spirit does not return to the Lord after death, but rather their spirit looks for another lodging place or residence.

Through the residue of these vile spirits, Satan uses them to continue to pollute the world. Fallen angels are spiritual beings. When you couple their vile spirit with the human spirit of women, we have a hybrid - some type of an alien entity. Due to the fallen nature of these giants, their alien spirit is manifest as demons. I believe that is why when people testify to having seen demons they often times describe them as alien type creatures having weird formations. Satan has been using Hollywood to prepare people for aliens, as in the movie ET. Now we are witnessing a barrage of zombie movies.

Needless to say, the seed of these fallen angels is a corrupt seed, versus the godly seed of Jesus Christ. I personally believe men that produce and create demonic movies must have seen these creatures; thus they portray them as vile, wicked aliens with profound distortions. Because many people desire the unseen world of evil, they are willing to yield themselves to Satan in many sinister ways. I have personally dealt with another realm and form of demonic activity about which many people have never heard.

During my pastorate of over 15 years in Charlotte, North Carolina, I once had a woman who confessed to me that she had sex with demons. I am not a counselor, nor do I profess to be one. I will only elaborate briefly and in a very shallow measure concerning the graphic details of this demonic experience that she shared with me. She conveyed to me that she had sexual relations *(intercourse)* with demons. She explained in graphic details their ungodly intimacy.

There are two demonic terms known as *incubus* and *succubus*. *Incubus* is the term used for male demons. These male demons purportedly seek out and lust to have sexual intercourse with women while women are either sleeping or awake. I believe when certain women cross the natural boundaries of humanity they are able to open themselves up to untold demonic activity. I believe that is what some evil women did prior to the Noachian flood. They opened up themselves to dark spiritual sexual activity. This can be true with anyone that submits himself or herself to the devil and not to Christ our Lord. *Succubus* is the exact opposite word, female demons having intercourse with male subjects. When male subjects open themselves up to *succubus,* they too have crossed an uncertain and forbidden boundary.

> Demons desire to possess a body because they are disembodied spirits.

Remember demons desire to possess a body because they are disembodied spirits. Many times in mental institutions, when people lose their mind and enter into the final state of psychosis, they often remove their clothing desiring to be perpetually naked. That is because demons are disembodied spirits and these poor demon-possessed souls finally take on the nature of the demonic spirit. The medical field would address this mental state as schizophrenia, a loss of reality. As children of God, we know it as demon possession.

I am firmly convinced that the demoniac at the Gadara was naked and wholly given over to psychosis and schizophrenia when he came to Jesus because he had lost his natural state of mind. He was a cutter, a term used for people who habitually cut themselves due to mental oppression. Although bound with fetters and chains, the demoniac was able to break free from them, and no man could tame or control him. I believe that he was naked because of what we read here in Mark 5:15, *"And they come to Jesus, and see him that was possessed with the devil, and had the legion, sitting, and clothed, and in his right mind (sound mind): and they were afraid."*

After Jesus delivered him, he was clothed and in his right mind. This modern generation would have medicated the man, but Jesus cast the demons out of him and set him free! I want to encourage each believer to be careful when dealing with prescription/pharmaceutical drugs. I addressed this issue because of what we read in Revelation 9:21, *"Neither repented they of their murders, nor of their sorceries, nor of their fornication, nor of their thefts."* The Greek word for sorceries is *pharmakeia* from which we get our English word *pharmacy.* We country folk call it a drugstore. There is a profound explosion in the use of mind-altering drugs such as Effexor, Zoloft, Prozac, Xanax, and a host of other drugs that are being promoted in this hour. I have discussed this with physicians who have shared with me that they are not sure what the drugs actually do to the neurons and receptors of the brain other than basically flat-line them.

Another medical term is *neurosis,* which only affects a part of the personality causing limited emotional disorder. It is often far less detrimental than psychosis. I am not here to condemn anyone but simply sharing the truth, please be careful with what you put into your body! I just want you to realize that drugs have the ability to lead people into the unseen world. That is why music, sex, theatrics, and Hollywood productions and inventions are often greatly enhanced by drugs. I am well aware that this may be hard for some of you to fathom, but that is why we are so adamant in preaching against sin. The more vile and wicked a person becomes the greater the satanic influence they will manifest within their lives.

Many people, though often times unknowingly, open themselves up to these demonic entities through drugs, alcohol, and promiscuity. Some Bible scholars believe that demons can be transferred sexually. That is why some people begin to seek deeper fleshly gratification once they have been exposed to that sinister and dark world. However, they often enter into a world in which they never intended to go or experience. Between the mind, soul and spirit there are dangerous dimensions that innocent people have often crossed, not knowing the end result. There is truly an unseen world ruled by darkness. That is why this Scripture is so apropos found in Ephesians 6:12, *"For we wrestle not against flesh and blood, but against principalities, against powers, against the rulers of the darkness of this world, against spiritual wickedness in high places."*

As Christians, we are sealed and insulated from much of

this activity, because of the blood of the Lamb. Furthermore, we seek him and not the things of this world. The Bible says that men make a mockery of sin thus; we must respect the powers of darkness for they are real. I do not fear satanic powers because, as a Holy Ghost filled believer; I have absolute authority over them. But we must recognize and respect their reality.

Paul himself had spiritual understanding of this dark sphere, for he declared emphatically in 2nd Corinthians 10:3 -5,

> *For though we walk in the flesh, we do not war after the flesh: for the weapons of our warfare are not carnal, but mighty through God to the pulling down of strong holds; casting down imaginations, and every high thing that exalteth itself against the knowledge of God, and bringing into captivity every thought to the obedience of Christ.*

The term *imaginations* in the Greek means *a purpose or thought within the mind not yet executed or acted upon.* When people are psychotic, they often admit they hear voices or someone or thing telling them to do something. That is demon possession, directing them to carry out particular tasks. The employee that shot and killed numerous people at the Naval Yard in Maryland some time ago said he too was hearing voices.

> Satan will shoot a fiery dart or heinous idea into your mind and try to coerce you to fulfill it.

Satan will shoot a fiery dart or heinous idea into your mind and try to coerce you to fulfill it. This is what Paul the apostle termed as seducing spirits. This is what was taking place prior to the Noachian flood adamantly. Satan and the fallen angels were seducing women to cross-forbidden boundaries and break through spiritual membranes God had placed within his creation. As someone has said, "Sin will take you further than you want to go, keep you longer than you want to stay, and cost you more than you really want to pay!"

As God's creation, we must seek spiritual edification rather than carnal gratification. There are realms and spheres where the godly should never desire to go or much less seek to encounter. These ungodly spheres have been totally polluted and contaminated by the fallen angels and demonic spirits. Fallen angels and demons continue to try to wreak havoc on humanity in this present day. Let us look closely here in Matthew 12:43-45,

> *When the unclean spirit is gone out of a man, he walketh through dry places, seeking rest, and findeth none. Then he saith, I will return into my house from whence I came out; and when he is come, he findeth it empty, swept, and garnished. Then goeth he, and taketh with himself seven other spirits more wicked than himself, and they enter in and dwell there: and the last state of that man is worse than the first. Even so shall it be also unto this wicked generation.*

From this passage, we see that demons seek rest or a place of residence and such rest can be found in a person's body. Demons also communicate one with another, because this demon sought others to come with him. They also seek fellowship one with another. Demons evidently can be more wicked than one another. One demon brought with him seven other demons 'more wicked than himself.' Their presence can only cause the state of a person to go, from bad to worse according to this passage.

When a man dies, his spirit returns the Lord, who gave it. We know this from Ecclesiastes 12:7, *"Then shall the dust return to the earth as it was: and the spirit shall return unto God who gave it."* We understand then, the remains of a man return to the ground from whence it came, but the spirit returns unto God, who gave it. But when these giants died, their bodies return to the earth, but their spirit, which is demonic, goes about seeking a place of habitation or residence. Let me reiterate, this is where, I believe, demonic spirits come from: they are the spirits of the deceased giants. The demons of these decedents desire a place of residence. We find this truth in Luke 8:30-33,

> *And Jesus asked him, saying, what is thy name? And he said, Legion: because many devils were entered in to him. And they besought him that he would not command them to go out into the deep (abyss). And there was there a herd of many swine feeding on the mountain: and they besought him that he would suffer them to enter into them. And he suffered them. Then went the devils out of the man, and entered into the swine: and the herd ran violently down a steep place into the lake, and were choked.*

The term *devils* in this passage is *diamonizomal* (Strong's: #1140) and in Greek, it means *a demonic being, a demon or supernatural spirit consisting of an evil nature.* Because of their evil nature, when these demons were cast out, they desired Jesus to suffer or tolerate them to enter into the swine. When he did, the swine immediately chose death by suicide. Demons can torment and vex earthly creatures to the degree of suicide and death. Peter, the apostle, told us that Satan himself goes about seeking whom he may devour.

Jude tells us that God destroyed Sodom and Gomorrah with fire, and they are an example of his judgment by their destruction to those who afterward should live an ungodly lifestyle. Jude is warning the church that they should never toy with sin. We have the identical prophetic warning in 2nd Peter 2:6, *"And turning the cities of Sodom and Gomorrah into ashes condemned them with an overthrow, making them an example unto those that after should live ungodly"*.

Contrary to modern theology, God will damn the wicked. He assures their eternal destruction, and their destiny will be hell. The psalmist declared in Psalms 9:17, *"The wicked shall be turned into hell and all the nations that forget God"*. While we are on the topic of hell, I want to share with you an exposition from Flavius Josephus with his tremendous discourse to the Greeks concerning Hades.

Now as to Hades, wherein the souls of the righteous *(we firmly believe that when the righteous die they go immediately to be with the Lord)* and unrighteous are detained, it is necessary to speak of it.

Hades is a place in the world not regularly finished; a subterraneous region, wherein the light of this world does not shine ... there must be in it perpetual darkness. This region is allotted as a place of custody for souls, in which angels are appointed as guardians to them, who distribute to them temporary punishments, agreeable to everyone's behavior and manners.

In this region, there is a certain place set apart, as a lake of unquenchable fire, where into, we suppose, no one hath hitherto been cast; but it is prepared for a day afore determined by God in which one righteous sentence shall deservedly be passed upon all men; when the unjust and those that have been disobedient to God, and have given honor to such titles as have been the main operations of the hands of men, as to God himself, shall be adjudged to this everlasting punishment, as having been the causes of defilement; while the just shall obtain an incorruptible and never-fading kingdom.

These are now, indeed, confined in Hades, but not at the same place wherein the unjust are confined. For there is one descent into this region, at whose gate we believe there stands an angel with an host; which gate, when those pass through that are conducted down by the angels appointed over the souls, they do not go the same way; but the just are guided to the right hand, and are led with him as, signed by the angels appointed over that place, unto a region of light, in which the just have dwelt from the beginning of the world; not constrained by necessity, but ever enjoying the prospect of the good things they see, and rejoice in the expectation of those new enjoyments, which will be particular to every one of them, and his esteeming those things beyond what we have here; with whom there is no place of toil, no burning heat, no piercing cold, nor are any briers there; but the countenance of the fathers and of the just, which they see always smiles upon them, while they wait for that rest and eternal new life in heaven, which is to succeed this region. This place we call the bosom of Abraham.

The commentary continues:

However, as to the unjust, they are dragged by force to the left-hand by the angel allotted for punishment, no longer going with a good will, but as prisoners driven by violence; to whom are sent the angels appointed over them to reproach them and threatened them with their terrible looks, and to thrust them still downwards. Now

those are angels that are set over the souls, drag them into
the neighborhood of hell itself; when they are hard by it,
continually hear the noise of it, and do not stand clear of
the hot vapor its self; but when they have a nearer view of
this spectacle, as of a terrible and exceeding great prospect
of fire, they are struck with a fearful expectation of a future judgment *(which is the great white throne judgment),*
and in effect punished there by: and not only so, but where
they see the place [or choir] of the fathers and of the just,
even hereby are they punished; for a *chaos (abyss)* deep
and large is fixed between them; in so that a just man that
hath compassion upon them cannot be admitted, nor can
one that is unjust if he were bold enough to attempt it,
pass over it.

This discourse by Josephus on hades continues in detail, offering a rare perspective from the era of the New Testament.

Hades, wherein the souls of men are confined until
a proper season, which God hath determined, when he
will make a resurrection of
all men from the dead, not
procuring a transmigration
of souls from one body to
another, but raising again
those very bodies, which you

> Jude warns the church that they should never toy with sin.

Greeks, seeking to be dissolved, do not believe[their res-
urrection]: but learned not to disbelieve it; for while you
believe that the soul is created, and yet is made immortal by God, according to the doctrine of Plato, and this
end time, be not incredulous; but believe that God is able,
would he have raised to life that body which was made as

a compound of the same elements, to make it immortal; for it must never be said of God, that he is able to do some things, and not able to do others. We have therefore believed that the body will be raised again; for although it be dissolved, it is not perished; for the Earth receives its remains, and preserves them; and while they are like seed, and are mixed among the more fruitful soil, they flourish, and what is sown is indeed sown bare again; but at the mighty sound of God the Creator, it will sprout up, and be raised in a clothed and glorious condition, though not before it has been dissolved, and mixed [with the earth]. So that we have not rationally believed the resurrection of the body; for although it be dissolved for a time on account of the original transgression, it exists still, and is cast into the earth and into a Potters furnace, in order to be formed again, not in order to rise again such as it was before, but in a state of purity, and so as never to be destroyed anymore; and to everybody shall its own soul be restored; and when it hath clothed itself with that body, it will not be subject to misery, but, being itself pure, it will continue with its pure body, and rejoice with it, with which it having walked righteously now in this world, and never having had it as a snare, it will receive it again with great gladness; but as for the unjust, they will receive their bodies not changed. All men, the just as well as the unjust, shall be brought before God the Word: for to him hath the Father committed all judgment; and he in order to fulfill the will of his Father, shall come as judge, whom we call Christ.

At this point, Josephus becomes rather pointed in his commentary, moving to challenge contemporary Greek mythology. It is reasonably clear, he is not proposing a mere 'alternate mythology,' but the historical perspective of his time.

For Minos *(a son of Zeus supposedly a supreme judge in the underworld after his death)* and Rhadmanthus *(also a supposedly judge of Greek mythology in the underworld,)* are not the judges, as you Greeks do suppose, but he whom God even the father hath glorified. This person, Jesus Christ exercising the righteous judgment of the father towards all men, hath prepared a just sentence for everyone, according to his works; at whose judgment seat when all men, and Angels and Demons shall stand, they will send forth with one voice, and say, just is thy judgment; he will bring a just sentence upon both parties, by giving generously to those that have done well an everlasting fruition; but allotting to the lovers of wicked works eternal punishment. To these belong the unquenchable fire, and that without end, and a certain fiery worm never dying, and not destroying the body, but continuing its eruption out of the body with never ceasing grief; neither will sleep give ease to these men, nor will the night afford them comfort; death will not free them from their punishment, nor will the interceding prayers of their kindred profit them; for the just are no longer seen by them, nor are they thought worthy of remembrance; but the just shall remember only the righteous actions whereby they have attained the heavenly kingdom, in which there is no sleep, no sorrow, no corruption, no care, no night, no day measured by time, no sun driven in his course along the circle of heaven by necessity; and measuring out the bounds and conversions of the seasons, for the better of illumination of the life of men; no moon decreasing and increasing, or introducing a variety of seasons, nor will she then moisten the earth; no burning sun."

What a tremendous commentary on Hades to say the least. What a powerful description Josephus gave concerning hell and the judgment of the just along with the unjust. Make no mistake; the lake of fire is the end result for all unrepentant sinners.

I trust it is your desire to live and walk in the power of the Holy Ghost so to never experience this place of the departed evil. There is a heaven to gain, and there is a hell to shun. Truly concerning both good and evil, eye hath not seen, nor ear heard, neither has entered to the heart of man the things which God hath prepared.

Jude 8

Likewise also these filthy dreamers defile the flesh, despised dominion, and speak evil of dignities.

These filthy dreamers are those certain men who have 'crept in unawares.' This verse also speaks to the sin of homosexuality. Jude 4 says these men 'turned the grace of God into lasciviousness.' That is certainly nothing less than a filthy dreamer. The idea of 'filthy dreamers' that 'defile their flesh' speaks directly to depravity and sodomy. Their sexual desires represent absolute perversion.

Sodomites seek to change, as well as challenge, the civil laws concerning marriage, which is between a man and a woman. Satan is a master at trying to redefine God's laws and boundaries when godly men should be seeking to reinforce them. Since the fall of Lucifer, all boundaries, both spiritual and earthly, have been corrupted. God Almighty established, in the very beginning of creation, that a marriage is between one man and one woman. One of my friends, now deceased, was Dr. Jim Forester, a former state senator, was able to get before the North Carolina people, on the state ballot, the proposition that affirmed marriage as between one man and one woman. It was not long after this law was ratified and passed by the constituents of North Carolina that Dr. Forester passed away. How greatly God used him to continue to be a deterrent to vile and wicked sinners.

God Almighty established marriage as between a man and a woman. We witness this truth in Genesis 2:21-25,

> And the Lord God caused a deep sleep to fall upon Adam, and he slept: and he took one of his ribs, and closed up the flesh instead thereof; and the rib, which the Lord God had taken from man, made he a woman, and brought her unto the man. And Adam said, this is now bone of my bones, and flesh of my flesh: she shall be called woman, because she was taken out of man. Therefore shall a man leave his father and his mother, and shall cleave unto his wife: and they shall be one flesh. And they were both naked, the man and his wife, and were not ashamed.

Sodomites challenge civil authority and laws because they desire the honor that God bestows upon marriage. The reason sodomites are so adamant in obtaining the right of marriage rather than civil unions is because they want and desire such honor. We read in Hebrews 13:4, *"Marriage is honorable in all, and the bed undefiled: but whoremongers and adulterers God will judge."* A man and his wife cannot possibly defile their bed for they are no longer twain but one flesh. No matter how hard they try, neither two men nor two women can become one flesh. That is because they are both the same sex, even though they seek to be joined. Spiritually, it takes a man and a woman to make a holy union, which is called marriage. Only people of the opposite sex, through marriage, can become one flesh

> Only people of the opposite sex, through marriage, can become one flesh and complete this godly union.

and complete this godly union. It is a 'God design' though men would seek to pervert it. Through the entirety of the universe, God's design is one of male and female: from keys to ignition switches, doors with locks, electrical plugs male and female, plumbing fittings male and female, hose pipes male and female, and cell phone charging cords male and female to the simplicity of a mail box, it's all male and female. It is a universal design by God. That is why two men cannot define marriage as a spiritual union because it is not God's design. It is totally impossible for men to be joined together to create a holy union. Neither can the two women.

The word whoremonger is *pornos* (Strong's: # 4205) and in Greek, it means *a male prostitute, a debauchee.* It also means *to be venal,* which simply means *to be brought or obtained by money for the purpose of corrupting one's influence.* The very act of sodomy is corruption within itself. Many homosexuals are very religious, even professing Christianity, which is an oxymoron with in itself.

On October 8, 2013, Reverend Gary Hall, chief ecclesiastical leader and executive officer of the National Cathedral in Washington, D.C. said in a sermon on that Sunday; that "homophobia" and "heterosexism" are sins. In his statement, he said, "In its wisdom, the church came to its senses and labeled both, racism and sexism as sinful. " How in the world is marriage between a man and a woman racist? What Mr. Hall fails to understand is the church is the body of the Lord Jesus Christ. For him to make this decision, he is operating outside of the body of the Lord Jesus Christ. He went on to say, "We must now have the courage to take the final step and call homophobia and heterosexism what they are," Hall said, "They are both sin and racism". My friend, that ecclesiastical leader, is an apostate and reprobate. He truly did take the final step in blaspheming God Almighty. Mr. Gary Hall violated the Holy Scripture, because he possesses no Holy Ghost conviction whatsoever within his conscience. In retrospect, he has called God a sinner, because God established heterosexism. Sex and marriage were designed for a man and a woman. This man certainly has no problem in despising dominion and speaking evil of dignities. Here, in our contemporary age, are those who have 'crept stealthy into the church.'

Some time ago, my wife and I went into a restaurant to have dinner. Moreover, while we were sitting in a restaurant eating dinner, we could not believe what we were about to witness. It was obvious; the two men who entered the restaurant and sat a few tables beyond us were flagrant and open homosexuals. They grasped one another's hands and entered into a rather lengthy prayer. I could not believe what I was witnessing. I was stunned. These two men actually believe, apparently, they can live such an ungodly lifestyle and supposedly communicate with God Almighty. They possess no conviction whatsoever concerning their sin and debasement. What we are witnessing today is a tremendous display of apostasy. I am not here to condemn, but it concerns me when I witness such of a display of sin with no remorse or conviction. You may say - that is being judgmental. However, if you witnessed a murder or knew someone was having an extramarital affair, how would you judge that? Liberal theology and sloppy grace has all but removed true conviction when it comes to dealing with sin. Due to political correctness, we have been seduced into being soft on sin today. May the Holy Ghost of God deal with those two men and bring them to the saving grace and the true knowledge of Christ our Lord.

All three: certain men, homosexuals, and fallen angels live in sensual and unbridled lust and are filled with rebellion. I regret to inform you but things will only get worse here in the end. You are going to witness an assault on Christianity as never before. Just as Jesus Christ said, 'They hated me without a cause, and they will hate you as well.' Jesus cried in John 15:18-19,

> *If the world hate you, ye know that it hated me before it hated you. If ye were of the world, the world would love his own; but because ye are not of the world, but I have chosen you out of the world, therefore, the world hateth you.*

We must never allow ourselves to feel the need for acceptance in this present world. If you bear your cross daily, you will be despised, rejected and castigated to no end. Satan sees the blood of the lamb upon your heart, thus making you a target. You do not have to go looking for trouble; trouble will come to your doorstep, often times, totally, unexpected.

Once the two angels sent by God entered into Lot's home, the sodomites came to him and adamantly troubled his house. Although he diligently pled with them to do no evil to the angelic visitors, their militant disposition was, we will do worse to you if we cannot *know* (*yada;* Strong's: #3045) them, which in Hebrew means to *sodomize them.* To this day, Sodomites defy and challenge God's plan concerning civil laws and government. Those sodomites challenged the very security of Lot's home with utter contempt. They sought to knock down the door of his house. Had the two angels not blinded them, they would have succeeded. Sodomites cannot procreate and replenish the earth. That alone defies God's plan of procreation, therefore; they make these civil challenges continually because they are of their father the devil.

They are driven by the spirit of the antichrist to break the laws established within our land. Although same-sex marriages are against the law in North Carolina, several news agencies have reported that numerous homosexual couples have gone to various county court houses trying to obtain marriage licenses. They openly attempt to repudiate the law. Lucifer challenged God Almighty before his fall, and that same spirit of rebellion permeates the hearts of these certain men, fallen angels, and homosexuals. This is the personification of rebelling against God's divine order.

Remember, it is God that created the heavens and the earth and placed everything in its order. Since the fall of Lucifer, he has tried to convolute and destroy God's supreme plan. Satan is ruthless, relentless, and untiring in his attack against God's plan for all the ages. This fallen nature of angels and mortal men still challenges the entire order of God.

Jude 9

Yet Michael the Archangel, when contending with the devil he disputed about the body of Moses, durst not bring against him a railing accusation, but said, the Lord rebuke thee.

After the death of Moses, Satan demanded that the body of Moses, the lawgiver, be given over to him for the death state. Remember, Satan still had power over death and the grave until the resurrection of Jesus Christ. We know this according to Hebrews 2:14,

Forasmuch then as the children are partakers of flesh and blood, he also himself likewise took part of the same; that through death he might destroy him that had the power of death, that is, the devil.

The reason that Jesus Christ had to take on the nature of a man, flesh and blood, was so that he could die a physical death. Although he was naturally born and incarnated in the flesh, he had royal blood flowing through his veins because he was conceived by the Holy Ghost. His blood had to be holy so that he might purge our sins. The blood of any child from conception comes from its father, and so it was with Jesus. Because of his Holy Spirit conception, he had royal blood coursing through his veins. Paul said in Hebrews 2:9, *"But we see Jesus, who was made that a little lower than the angels for the suffering of death, crowned with glory and honor; that he by the grace of God should taste death for every man."* We now understand why Jesus had to be made lower than angels, so that he could die a natural death.

Satan desired the body of Moses because he could then take his body and memorialize it so that all of Israel might live in perpetual idolatry. Therefore, God hid his body, when he buried him. Satan sought untiringly to find his body to the point of spiritual confrontation with Michael the Archangel. Jude says that Michael and the devil were contending or disputing with each other over the body of Moses. So rather than furthering the dispute and offering proof over the body of Moses, Michael simply said Satan, "The Lord rebuke thee." Michael understood that bringing a railing accusation against Satan would be useless. As I previously stated, Satan can never outgun or out man God Almighty! Christ has now conquered death and hell; thus, Moses will be resurrected at the second advent of Christ our Lord. Even Michael, the Archangel, understands the power of Christ and the power of his holy name.

> We now understand why Jesus had to be made lower than angels, so that he could die a natural death.

Jude 10

But these speak evil of those things which they know not: but what they know naturally, as brute beast, in those things they corrupt themselves.

When Jude used the phrase, "but these speak evil," he refers to the 'certain men' who have 'crept in unawares,' fallen angels, and sodomites. All three entities perpetually speak evil of God and his word. They all possess a natural hostility toward God and his spiritual authority. Again, Jude describes them as brute beast living by fleshly lusts and perverted instincts. They are truly the personification of corrupt beings. These certain men and sodomites live in the perpetuity of their flesh. All they know is totally flawed because they only dwell within the confines and realm of carnality. This is why demonic spirits and fallen angels appeal to these certain men and the sodomites who have crept into the church. It is all about fleshly gratification, and they are wholly given over to it. What a grave tragedy to be described as a 'brute beast.'

Mr. Gary Hall, the chief ecclesiastical leader and executive officer of the National Cathedral, is the personification of this scripture passage. In all reality, he condemned, as well as blasphemed, God Almighty, by calling heterosexism and anyone who opposes sodomy to be a sinner. It is high time that every pulpit start preaching against sin. When will the supposed men of God realize that this sin is destroying this nation and every family within it? It has nothing to do with education or social status; it has to do with an unrepentant heart and a life filled with sin. We must abandon political correctness and embrace spiritual and doctrinal soundness. Truth never diminishes in spite of men. Men can hammer the truth, profane the truth and debate the truth. But in the end, it is still the truth.

Paul cried aloud in 2nd Corinthians 13:8, *"For we can do nothing against the truth, but for the truth."* His truth remains the same! When men walk in the counsel of the ungodly, they err profusely. We were admonished by the psalmist never to walk in the counsel of the ungodly. We read in Psalms 1:1, *"Blessed is the man that walketh not in the counsel of the ungodly, nor standeth in the way of sinners, nor sitteth in the seat of the scornful."* The psalmist also declared in Psalms 12:8, *"The wicked walk on every side, when the vilest men are exalted".*

> Truth never diminishes in spite of men. Men can hammer the truth, profane the truth and debate the truth. But in the end, it is still the truth.

As long as we continue to promote sin, we will witness vile men continue to be exalted in this nation. The reason there is so much sorrow in our land today is because the wicked have been exalted. We read in Proverbs 29:2, *"When the righteous are in authority, the people rejoice: but when the wicked beareth rule, the people mourn."* When the righteous are in authority, they do not oppress the people, because they do honorable things in behalf of the people. But when the wicked are in authority, the Bible says, the people will mourn. Look at this nation presently, at the mass numbers of foreclosed houses, the lack of good jobs, and the enormity of true unemployment, which is reportedly in the neighborhood of 25 percent. Regretfully, things are not going to get any better, they will only get worse. Everyone reading this book must get his or her house in order. The storm is about to break upon us all. Anyone who believes that things are going to get better without our turning to God is absolutely deceived. This nation is being plunged into total chaos as well as disorder. Unless there is true repentance in this nation, we will remain in this downward spiral. The spiritual leadership of this nation is all but gone. It is truly my heart's desire to see and an old-fashioned move of the power of God Almighty. But this will never take place, until the pulpits in America are once again endued with power from on high.

I challenge every one of you reading this book, to seek the Lord for a fresh outpouring of the Holy Spirit within your personal life. I trust that you will also pursue the Lord of glory for a fresh anointing upon your life. The Psalmist declared in Psalms 92:10, *"I shall be anointed with fresh oil."* There is only one element that can break the yoke of bondage upon this nation, and it is the anointing of the Holy Spirit. We read in Isaiah 10:27, *"And the yoke shall be destroyed the because of the anointing."* If men will pray, God will answer. For the psalmist said in Psalms 34:15, *"The eyes of the Lord are upon the righteous, and his ears are open unto their cry".*

If the righteous will cry out to the Lord God of Abraham, he will hear us. If we fail to cry out, then there is nothing for God to hear and no plea for him to answer. I challenge every one of you to a deeper and more consecrated prayer life in the coming days. Jude goes on to say that these brute beasts will only continue to corrupt themselves relative to the things they know naturally. These men have not the spirit of God, so they are unable to understand the deep spiritual things of God. We must daily remind ourselves to be carnally minded is death, but to be spiritually minded is life and peace. The Holy Ghost brings true placidity.

Jude 11

Woe unto them! For they have gone in the way of Cain, and ran greedily after the error of Balaam for reward, and perished in the gainsaying of Core.

Jude screams adamantly at all of the apostates, "Woe". Woe simply means great will be your grief. Jude says that some will go in the way of Cain. This proves they are apostates, for they have gone into apostasy by being like Cain and conforming to a religion rather than Jesus Christ. Paul said in Romans 12:1-2,

I beseech you therefore, brethren, by the mercies of God, that ye present your bodies a living sacrifice, holy, acceptable unto God, which is your reasonable service. And be not conformed to this world: but be ye transformed by the renewing of your mind, that ye may prove what is that good, and acceptable, and perfect, will of God.

Paul was well aware, if men did not submit themselves to God as a living sacrifice, they would easily be conformed to this present world. The spirit of the world seeks to change us all. Therefore, the Lord said in Malachi 3:6, *"For I am the Lord, I change not."* Paul admonishes the children of God to be transformed by the renewing of their mind. Paul reemphasized the renewing of the mind found here in Ephesians 4:23, *"And be renewed in the spirit of your mind."* For a man's mind to be renewed, his mind must be subjected to the Holy Spirit. If an individual's mind is never transformed by the Spirit of God and never renewed by the Holy Spirit, he lives in a perpetual state of hostility towards God.

These men are never Spirit-led but rather they grieve the Holy Ghost by their perversion. They refuse to believe that redemption is only by the blood of the Lamb. They somehow perceive that, through their own vain works, they shall be saved. They demonstrate a lack of faith in the vicarious and efficacious work that Jesus wrought on the cross. Just as Paul addressed the Galatians and questioned how could they be so quickly removed unto another gospel; he, therefore, indicted them in writing by saying unto them, "Who hath bewitched or seduced you?"

The error of Balaam was that of greed, covetousness, and vile brinksmanship. We witness the spirit of Balaam every day on so-called Christian television. I have never witnessed so much rhetorical jargon advocating prosperity as I do today. It seems as though everyone has become a prosperity preacher. I would rather have Jesus Christ than all the riches of this present world. We are cautioned, as well as admonished, that if we have

> Men will be either con-*tent* or discon-*tent*-ed; which *tent* will you choose to live under?

food and clothing, then we should be content. I like what Paul, the apostle, emphasized in Philippians 4:11, *"Not that I speak in respect of want: for I have learned, in whatsoever state I am, there with to be content."* Men will be either con-*tent* or discon-

tent-ed; which *tent* will you choose to live under?

Jude is furthermore led by the Holy Ghost to mention another rebel whose name was Korah. Korah despised truth, authority and spiritual leadership. He challenged God's authority, given by God to both Moses and Aaron. Korah possessed a spirit of rebellion, and so do these others; the certain men, the fallen angels, and the sodomites. Again, all three entities personify rebellion and the repudiation of God's holy word. These three men that Jude addresses here speak to the same disposition of the fallen angels, the false prophets, and the homosexuals. These three men, identified by Jude, represent all who oppose the spirit of Jesus Christ.

Both Moses and Aaron speak of the coming Messiah. Moses was a type of Christ, for he was a deliverer. Aaron was a type of Christ by being the high priest. Korah was rebelling against the man who would deliver him, Moses; and Aaron, the high priest representing Jesus Christ, who would save him. Jesus Christ is the high priest for all mankind. We read in Hebrews 4:14, *"Seeing then that we have a great high priest, that is passed into the heavens, Jesus the Son of God, let us hold fast our profession"*. It is imperative that every child of God hold fast their profession of faith, no matter what they may have to face. Jesus is the only one that can bring men to God the father. That is why Jesus said in John 14:6, *"I am the way, the truth, and the life: no man cometh unto the father, but by me."*

Never before have we witnessed so many ministers teaching that there are multiple ways to enter into the kingdom of God. One of the largest Christian television networks is advocating Chrislam. Chrislam is Christianity and Islam, supposedly synthesized. The very word Chrislam typifies rebellion and apostasy. Solomon admonished us in Proverbs 14:12, *"There is a way which seemeth right unto a man, but the end thereof are the ways of death."* If it is not God's way, which is the way of the cross, then it is an evil way. Just because a way may seem right unto a man does not mean it is the right way.

Again, we read in Hebrews 8:1-2,

> *Now of the things which we have spoken this is the sum: we have such a high priest, who is set on the right hand of the throne of the Majesty in the heavens; a minister of the sanctuary, and of the true tabernacle which the Lord pitched, and not man.*

The sum of the matter is that Jesus Christ is the only Savior. The earthly tabernacle that Moses pitched was given by revelation of the true tabernacle which God the Father had already established in heaven. All who repudiate, challenge, and gainsay will utterly perish in the end. I trust that we all will be quick to repent if we err or sin in grieving the Holy Spirit of God in any way.

Jude 12

———◆———

These are spots in your feast of charity, when they feast with you, feeding themselves without fear: clouds they are without water, carried about of winds; trees whose fruit withereth, without fruit, twice dead, plucked up by the roots.

Jude declared that these apostates are spots or hidden rocks within your love feast. 'When they feast' or 'fellowship with' the people of God, they are like shepherds who pastor their flock. However, these men are very subtle, and they actually seek to devour and fleece the flock though pretending to feed the flock. They are not recognized as hirelings, though they truly are hirelings. Jesus describes them as 'wolves in sheep's clothing.' They always seek self-gratification and not the spiritual edification of others. They are 'clouds without water.' They never bring copious amounts of refreshing truth and doctrine to the body of the Lord Jesus Christ by the Holy Ghost.

Again, Peter, the apostle, also dealt with this same issue in 2nd Peter 2:17, *"These are wells without water, clouds that are carried with a tempest: to whom the midst of darkness is reserved for ever."* They are described as 'wells without water' which cannot irrigate the souls of men with the water of the precious word. Israel has also faced the same dilemma. We read in 2nd Chronicles 15:3, *"Now for a long season Israel hath been without the true God, and without a teaching priest, and without law"*. The term teaching here is *yara* (Strong's: #3384), in Hebrew, it means *to irrigate, to moisten, or to give water.* For that reason, Israel withered away and fell into apostasy, and we are witnessing the same thing in the modern church today.

The preaching of God's word is a well of salvation for all men. Regretfully, there has become a tremendous famine of the word of God. Because of that, denominations, ministries, churches and ministers are truly withering away spiritually. Jude declared that these charlatans were carried about by a certain kind of wind. This kind of wind speaks of false doctrine. Tornadic winds of heresy have blown across the modern church today, and the destruction is unfathomable. This nation has witnessed tornadoes that have totally eviscerated entire cities, but false doctrine has done far greater damage, because, without repentance, that damage is eternal and irreparable. The apostles knew false doctrine would ultimately blow across the church and cause great harm, and that is why Paul said in Ephesians 4:14,

> *That we henceforth be no more children, tossed to and fro, and carried about with every wind of doctrine, by the sleight (the word sleight in the Greek speaks of loaded dice; you can never win with the loaded dice of false doctrine) of men, and cunning craftiness, whereby they lie in wait to deceive.*

Both Paul and Jude warned us of these certain men who have crept in unawares who seek to damage the body of the Lord Jesus Christ. These false messengers lie in wait to deceive every soul they possibly can. Jude describes these false messengers as 'trees whose fruit has withered' and other trees that are totally without fruit. Jude describes two classes of false prophets, those whose fruit has withered and those who are totally fruitless.

Those without fruit are undoubtedly cursed and do not even realize it. We recognize this truth from Jesus here in Matthew 21:18-20,

> Now in the morning as he returned into the city, he hungered. And when he saw a fig tree in the way, he came to it, and found nothing there on, but leaves only, and said unto it, let no fruit grow on thee henceforth forever. And presently the fig tree withered away. And when the disciples saw it, they marveled saying, how soon is the fig tree withered away!

The fig tree speaks of the nation Israel, but it also speaks of false prophets who have no fruit of the Spirit of Christ operating within their lives. Because of no fruit, Jesus cursed the unfruitful tree. And quickly, it withered away. These also have withered because they are no longer attached to the vine, which is Jesus Christ. Some have been pruned by the Holy Ghost, and others are now cut off from Jesus Christ, which is the real tree of life. Hear the words of Christ as he expounds on this subject in John 15:1-6,

Withering occurs because you are no longer attached to the vine, which is Jesus Christ.

> I am the true vine, and my father is the husbandman. Every branch in me that beareth not fruit he taketh away: and every branch that beareth fruit, he purgeth it, that it may bring forth more fruit. Now ye are clean through the word which I have spoken unto you. Abide in me, and I in you. As the branch cannot bear fruit of its self, except it abide in the vine; no more can ye, except ye abide in me. I am the

vine, ye are the branches: he that abideth in me, and I in him, the same bringeth forth much fruit: for without me ye can do nothing. If a man abide not in me, he is cast forth as a branch, and is withered; and men gather them, and cast them into the fire, and they are burned.

If a minister, ministry or person is not bearing the fruit of Jesus Christ, then it will be taken away. The tree may be standing, as the one Jesus found here, but without fruit. Jesus declared that these withered and dead branches would be ultimately gathered and cast into the fire where they would burn for eternity. Jude went on to say that these men were twice dead. What exactly does it mean to be twice dead? Once dead in their trespasses, they had been born-again. But now they have rebelled and left their place of redemption, just as the fallen angels, so now they are estranged from Christ for a second time. They have turned back to a life of sin along with the pollutions of this present world, and that makes them twice dead.

They are apostates who have abandoned the faith once delivered to the saints. No sinner before salvation can be an apostate. Apostates are those who have been born again and have abandoned or been seduced from the faith. Those that have fallen away have now become vile, to say the least. We read here in 2nd Peter 2:22, *"But it is happened unto them according to the true proverb, the dog is turned to his own vomit again; and the sow that was washed to her wallowing in the mire."* The *mire*, simply put, is *mud*. The Greek word translated *wallowing* means *to be rolling about in filth*. These souls have returned again, a second time, to their own vomit from which they were once delivered. How deceptive sin can be in seducing men to return to their old destructive ways. That old saying is absolutely true, "We now have pigs in the parlor."

I never fail to be amazed at how graphic the Holy Ghost can be in describing those who have returned to the world. Peter is under the unction of the Holy Ghost to write about a dog's vomit and pigs wallowing in filth. Do you not think that the Holy Ghost is trying to convey a stern warning, through Peter the apostle, to the end time church?

I trust your desire is to live and walk in the paths of righteousness for his name's sake.

Jude 13

Raging waves of the sea, foaming out there shame; wandering stars, to whom is reserved (kept from escaping) the blackness of darkness forever.

Jude says that these certain men, fallen angels, and homosexuals are like *raging waves,* which simply means that they are wild and completely out-of-control. The rage is evidence by the ferocity of their evil desires, works and intentions. The Greek implies that they can be potentially, as wild as a herd of cattle when stampeding. Their *foaming shame* speaks of their vile passions that are completely unbridled. Their shame is so disgraceful that it should be shunned due to the dishonor it brings.

When men lose their sensitivity to the Holy Ghost, there is nothing they will not do, once they are past spiritual consciousness. Other than the word of God and the Holy Spirit, the greatest level of authority in a person's life is their conscience. Once the conscience has become seared or grossly defiled, men easily cross certain boundaries. That is the theme and motif of the book of Jude. Paul, the apostle, gave us this profound warning found in Ephesians 4:19, *"Who being past feeling have given themselves over unto lasciviousness, to work all uncleanness with greediness."* The phrase *past feeling* means they have grieved out the spirit and have become apathetic. The word *uncleanness* in the Greek speaks of *filth in a natural or physical sense;* it denotes *an unnatural pollution* whether acted out by one's self or with another person.

As *wandering stars,* they bring forth no genuine light for direction, guidance or spiritual navigation. They are reserved for a sorrowful judgment with the end result being truly unfavorable. They are reserved and kept from escaping the blackness of darkness forever. Darkness is reserved for these wandering stars, in part, because they were created to have been a genuine star and guiding light. In ancient times, stars were used for navigation because of their specific placement in the heavens. The Scriptures tell us in Genesis 1:14, *"And God said, let there be lights in the firmament of the heaven to divide the day from the night; and let them be for signs, and for seasons, and for days, and years."*

It is Satan's desire to tamper with the cosmos, both physically and spiritually. The term *reserved* in the Greek means, *they are placed in a fortress to be guarded and detained in custody in which there is no escaping.* This blackness of darkness is sheer gloom, filled with doom and misery forever and ever, in perpetuity.

Jude 14

And Enoch also, the seventh from Adam, prophesied of
these, saying, behold, the Lord cometh with ten thousands
of his saints.

In this passage, Jude quotes a direct prophecy from the
book of Enoch. Some church fathers recognized the book of
Enoch and its authenticity. However, the book was not affirmed as part of the canon. This prophecy, given by Enoch,
describes the second advent of Christ our Lord, coming with
ten thousands of his saints.

As I have previously written, as well as expounded in my
other books, neither Enoch nor Jude speaks of a pre-tribulation rapture. It is man's erroneous teachings that advocate a
pre-tribulation rapture. None of the apostles of our Lord Jesus Christ ever made a delineation between the rapture and
the second advent of Jesus Christ. All of the apostles of our
Lord Jesus Christ taught that the rapture of the church, the
second advent of Christ and the first resurrection, are all the
same event rolled up in one. Again, let it be clear that there
will only be one second coming of Christ. When he returns,
he will come with all of his saints. We read in Hebrews 9:28,

"So Christ was once offered to bear the sins of many, and unto them that look for him shall he appeared a second time without sin unto salvation".

When Jesus returns, he only brings with him the sainted dead and not the living Saints, because we read in 1st Thessalonians 4:14, *"For if we believe that Jesus died and rose again, even so them also which sleep in Jesus will God bring with him."* Paul did not say he would bring the living back with him, but the dead. The living shall be caught up together with them to meet the Lord in the air. Jesus Christ is only going to bring the *sainted dead* with him at his sec-

> The living shall be caught up together with them to meet the Lord in the air.

ond coming and we which are alive and remain - *those who have survived* the great tribulation - shall be caught up together with them in the clouds to meet the Lord in the air.

Friend, many saints of God will survive the great tribulation and be alive at the coming of Christ. These saints are the ones that we read about here in 1st Thessalonians 3:13, *"To the end he may establish your hearts unblamable in holiness before God, even our Father, at the coming of our Lord Jesus Christ with all his saints".* We have been taught that the armies in Revelation 19:14 are the saints of God. The truth is the armies in heaven are angels who will return with Christ at his second coming.

Let us do a quick examination in providing evidentiary proof that the armies coming with Christ from heaven are his holy angels. We read in Revelation 19:14, *"And the armies which were in heaven followed him up on white horses, and clothed in fine linen, white and clean".* The term *armies* here in the Greek speaks of a body of troops, a military campaign, an army, i.e., the angels, the celestial luminaries, a heavenly host. We find this same heavenly host of angelic luminaries as they return with Christ at his second advent in 2nd Thessalonians 1:7-8,

> And to you who are troubled rest with us, when the Lord Jesus shall be revealed from heaven with his mighty angels (powerful angels), in flaming fire taking vengeance on them that know not God, and that obey not the gospel of our Lord Jesus Christ; who shall be punished with everlasting destruction from the presence of the Lord, and from the glory of his power; when he shall come to be glorified in his saints, and to be admired in all them that believe (we which are alive and remain at his second advent) because our testimony among you was believed in that day.

Notice very closely with me, this is at the second coming of Christ when he will come to be glorified in the saints. It is at the second advent of Christ that he glorifies the saints. Paul made this teaching very clear in Colossians 3: 4, "When Christ, who is our life, shall appear, then shall ye also appear with him in glory".

The saints of God will appear with him in his glory or be transformed at his second coming. Peter, the apostle, also taught the same doctrine for we read in 1st Peter 1:7,

> That the trial of your faith, being much more precious than of gold that perisheth, though it be tried with fire, might be found unto praise and honor and glory at the appearing of Jesus Christ.

The believer will be a participant and recipient of the glory of Christ at his second advent. Peter reiterated this same doctrine and gave the child of God hope when facing grievous troubles and trials. We read in 1st Peter 4:12-13,

Beloved, think it not strange concerning the fiery trial which is to try you, as though some strange thing happened unto you: but rejoice in as much as ye are partakers of Christ's sufferings; that, when his glory shall be revealed, ye may be glad also with exceeding joy.

Both the glory of Christ and the glory that the child of God will partake will be manifest at his second coming and advent. This is certainly one event and experience you do not want to miss. The signs of the times tell us his coming is near my friend.

Jude 15

To execute judgment upon all, and to convince all that are ungodly among them of all their ungodly deeds which they have ungodly committed, and all their hard speeches which ungodly sinners have spoken against him.

The judgment Jude speaks of here is one of separation and sundering for eternal separation from the presence of God. This judgment will commence when he executes judgment upon all that have opposed him. In this verse, Jude uses the term ungodly four times. He says that Christ will convince or convict all of their ungodliness. Jude is not only recognizing but also emphasizing the ungodliness that will grow exponentially in the last days. The Lord will judge all in the earth at his second advent. His judgment will be for the purpose of convicting all that are ungodly of their ungodly deeds, their ungodly acts, and declaring emphatically that they are ungodly sinners.

This correlates exactly with Paul's definition at the Second Advent of Christ found here in 2nd Thessalonians 1:7-10,

And to you who are troubled rest with us, when the Lord Jesus shall be revealed from heaven with his mighty angels, in flaming fire taking vengeance on them that know not

God, and that obey not the gospel of our Lord Jesus Christ: who shall be punished with everlasting destruction from the presence of the Lord, and from the glory of his power; when he shall come to be glorify in his saints, and to be admired in all them that in that day.

I never fail to be amazed at the harmony of the gospels and the epistles of the apostles of our Lord Jesus Christ. These entities: the certain men, the fallen angels, and the sodomites were godly at one time, but now they are all deemed to be ungodly. The Greek word translated *ungodly* tends to show *they were at one time reverent and pious but now they are irreverent and impious or wicked.* Were not all the angels godly at their creation, do not all, or most ministers start out godly in their beginning: are not all homosexuals straight until someone introduces them to sodomy? I know that many in the homosexual community say, "God made me this way!" However, that is like saying, "God made me a drunkard, an adulterer, a fornicator, or even a bank robber". God does not make anyone evil. Men become evil because of whom they serve and to whom they surrender. Being good or evil comes down to a choice. You can choose to be good at this very moment or choose to do something evil. Again, it boils down to a choice. Men become products of the things to which they subject themselves. The psalmist David understood the power of sin and its dominion. Thus, he prayed in Psalms 119:133, *"Order my steps in thy word: and let not any iniquity have dominion over me."* The word *dominion* in Hebrew means *to govern, permit, or to have lordship over.* Paul, when writing to the church at Rome, a city inundated with sodomy, gave divine revelation and understanding about sin and what happens if we subject ourselves to it. Paul says plainly in Romans 6:12-14,

> Let not sin therefore reign in your mortal body, that ye should obey it in the lusts thereof. Neither yield ye your members as instruments of unrighteousness unto sin: but yield yourselves unto God, as those that are alive from the dead, and your members as instruments of righteousness unto God. For sin shall not have dominion over you: for ye are not under the law, but under grace.

Whatever we yield ourselves to is what we become and will be what we serve. Jesus declared adamantly in Matthew 6:24, "No man can serve two masters: for either he will hate the one, and love the other; or else he will hold to the one, and despise the other. You cannot serve God and mammon." Whatever we yield ourselves to, will no doubt have dominion, authority and lordship over our lives.

Remember, the Bible declares emphatically that man was created in the image and likeness of God. But that image was marred by sin. So we read in Genesis 5:3, "And Adam lived a hundred and thirty years, and begat a son in his own likeness, after his image; and called his name Seth". Notice the difference, Seth was made after the image of Adam and not in the likeness of God. Adam was reproducing his image in Seth, which was a fallen or a marred image, rather than the image and likeness of God his creator. Jesus said in John 8:34, "Verily, verily, I say unto you, whosoever committed sin is the servant of sin." If you live in sin, you are the servant of sin.

The Surgeon General determined in 1976 that homosexuality was a learned behavior. Paul established that truth for he declared in Romans; they *leave* or *forsake* and abandon what is natural. Paul declared in Romans 1:26-27,

For this cause God gave them up until vile affections: for even their women did change the natural use into that which is against nature: And likewise also the men, leaving the natural use of the woman, burned in their lust one toward another; men with men working that which is unseemly, and receiving in themselves that recompense of their error which was meet.

When men change the truth of God into a lie, worship and serve the creature more than the creator, it is at that point and time God allows them to be given over to their own vile passions and affections. Remember, it was fallen angels that taught men the deprivation and depravity of homosexuality. All angels are male in gender and because they live eternally, God did not create female angels because there was no need for procreation among them. Those angels broke through the bounds that God had set for them. I am firmly convinced that, in their rebellion, they sodomized one another, seeking self-gratification.

Let me establish a very profound point. Most every person that has ever indulged in any type of sin was introduced to sin by someone else. Someone introduced them to pornography; someone presented them with their first joint or line of cocaine, and someone gave them their first alcoholic beverage. It is the nature of fallen angels to introduce men to ungodly acts and thus it is the nature of fallen men to introduce others to that same immorality. No, 10, 11, 12, or 13-year-old child understands where to go and get drugs or alcohol unless it is already in their homes. Even in the confines of promiscuity, someone with some pre-marital sexual experience introduces the innocent to those ungodly acts of sin. That is the very reason we are so adamant and ardent in preaching against sin. The word of God with Holy Ghost conviction is a tremendous deterrent to sin. Every issue that I am addressing in this book of Jude derives around sin, perversion, and wickedness. This perversion was all passed on by Satan's rebellion and fallen angels.

Having raised four children, I never introduced my children to any sin or wickedness knowingly, but their friends or so-called friends, introduced them to sin and immorality. As parents, our responsibility is to teach our children not to lie, steal, or commit any ungodly action. The fallen nature is already within them, passed on from our loins, and therefore we must seek to deter their sinful nature. That is exactly the same way you probably came to the knowledge of sin and evil! Someone offered you with the opportunity

> Although all men have the tendency and propensity to sin, Satan only comes to enhance that probability and proclivity.

to sin against God. Although all men have the tendency and propensity to sin, Satan only comes to enhance that probability and proclivity. Satan was the one who introduced Adam and Eve to their sin and debasement. They were the epitome of innocence and knew nothing about sin, but their introduction to sin and separation from God was through that subtle lying serpent that seduced them.

Remember, Jesus said that Satan was a liar from the beginning. We read in John 8: 44,

> *Ye are of your father the devil, and the lust of your father you will do. He was a murderer from the beginning, and abode not in the truth, because there is no truth in him. When he speaketh a lie, he speaketh on his own: for he is a*

liar, and the father of it.

Sin and its origin can always be traced back to Lucifer. We know that according to the Scripture found in Ezekiel 28:15, *"Thou wast perfect in thy ways from the day that thou wast created, till iniquity was found in thee."* Because of sin, all of these entities are now ungodly, wicked, and irreverent. Just like Satan, they have all declared hard speeches against the Lord of glory and have, for the most part, blasphemed God Almighty.

The final act of rebellion through the Antichrist will speak evil things and blasphemies against the Lord of glory. May you strive and contend to live a godly life in this nefarious hour. Jesus said, "Blessed are the pure in heart, for they shall see God." It will take genuine purity without corruption to see the King of glory. I pray that your heart is fixed, and you are determined to live in his grace and mercy. The way is far straighter and narrower than most people believe.

Jude 16

*These are murmurers, complainers, walking after their own
lust; and their mouth speaking great swelling words, having
men's persons in admiration because of advantage.*

Jude describes the character and spiritual disposition of
the ungodly as being murmurers and complainers. Because of this, they are the ones who walk after their own
ungodly lust. They use much flattery to seduce and draw the
souls of men into their snares and ruthless traps. They show
respect for ungodly gain because they never acquire enough
to satisfy their souls. They grumble and complain profusely
because they never have enough to feed their carnal desires.

The truth is, the soul of man is so vast only God Almighty
can fill that void and vacuity. These ungodly certain men flat-
ter people and show great respect for the purpose of making
money and gaining their loyalty. They are known for ignor-
ing the Holy Ghost and walking after the flesh. Regrettably,
these men never operate in the fluidity of the Holy Spirit. We
rarely see a move of God coupled with Holy Ghost conviction
through these men in bringing sinners to repentance. Let me
be clear, the Holy Ghost cannot operate fluidly through car-

nage and carnality. The disposition of these certain men is one
of ungodliness, greed, and covetousness.

Paul describes the nature of these men in much detail here
in Romans 8:5-8,

> For they that are after the flesh to mind the things of the
> flesh; but they that are after the spirit the things of the spir-
> it. For to be carnally minded is death; but to be spiritually
> minded is life and peace. Because the carnal mind is enmi-
> ty against God: for it is not subject to the law of God, nei-
> ther indeed can be. So then they that are in the flesh cannot
> please God.

When men live in the flesh, there is a natural hostility and
anger toward God. Therefore, death will ultimately reign in
their lives. These men really know nothing about true riches
and divine provision from God alone. We are told, 'Having
food and raiment, let us be content.' These men seek to seduce
people by flattery with great swelling words. These men seek
admiration to have an advantage or upper hand over the innocent. May we all beware of flattering lips and deceitful words
they are truly a snare to catch the souls of men.

Jude 17

━━━━━━◆━━━━━━

*But, beloved, remember ye the words which were spoken be-
fore of the apostles of our Lord Jesus Christ.*

Jude is emphatic in where our faith must be placed. It must
be placed in the work of the cross, and that is fully understood by 'the words which were spoken by the apostles of
our Lord Jesus Christ.' There is a vast difference and distinc-
tion between *worldly apostles and the apostles of our Lord Jesus
Christ.*

Peter, the apostle, also recognized the power of the inspired word of God given to the apostles of our Lord Jesus
Christ. We read in 2nd Peter 1:21, *"For the prophecy came
not in old time by the will of man: but holy men of God spake
as they were moved by the Holy Ghost."* Peter, directed by the
Holy Ghost, purposely opened his epistles by declaring that he
was an apostle of our Lord Jesus Christ. No less than nineteen
times, Paul, the apostle, addressed himself as 'an apostle of our
Lord Jesus Christ'. The Holy Ghost felt it was very necessary
and needful to establish their apostleship when writing to the
churches. Therefore, they were inspired by the Holy Spirit to
record that spiritual milestone.

Because there was so much heresy, fallacious teachings, and false letters circulating among the people, the Holy Ghost led these men to clarify and verify their apostleship in the Lord Jesus Christ. Though Jude did not open his epistle by declaring his apostleship, he did, however, tell us to *remember* the words of the apostles of our Lord Jesus Christ. Throughout the entirety of the New Testament, Paul, Peter, as well as Jude, who were apostles of our Lord Jesus Christ, understood that there would be a plethora of false prophets and apostles in the last days.

Jesus himself gave dire warnings of what the child of God should expect in the last days. He declared in Matthew 24:11, *"And many false prophets shall rise, and shall deceive many."* Paul, the apostle, was compelled by the Holy Ghost to convey the same message to the church at Corinth. We read in 2nd Corinthians 11:13-15,

> *For such are false apostles, deceitful workers, transforming themselves into the apostles of Christ. And no marvel; for Satan himself is transformed into an angel of light. Therefore it is no great thing if his ministers also be transformed as the ministers of righteousness; whose end shall be according to their works.*

Again, we see how adamant Peter, the apostle, was in warning the church just as Jude did for we read in 2nd Peter 2:1-3,

> *But there were false prophets also among the people, even as there shall be false teachers among you, who privily shall bring in damnable heresies, even denying the Lord that bought them, and bring upon themselves swift destruction. And many shall follow their pernicious ways; by reason of whom the way of truth shall be evil spoken of. And through covetousness shall they with feigned (plastic) words make*

merchandise (mart or mall) of you: whose judgment now of a long time lingereth not, and their damnation slumbereth not.

The term *feigned* means *artificial and plastic.* The Greek word is *plastos* from which we get our English word *plastic.* Who would have believed, since the 20th century, we would be witnessing the degree of apostasy and heresy we are witnessing in this present day?

These men are all plastic and from the same mold or frame. We call them cookie-cutter preachers. There was a day when you could walk into almost any Protestant church and sense the power of God and the awesome presence of the Holy Ghost. Regretfully, that is no longer true and for the most part, the Holy Ghost is no longer felt even in most Pentecostal church-es. Isn't it amazing how accurate the word of God is today, though it was recorded over nineteen hundred years ago? Oh, how I long for a freshet and flood of the Holy Ghost today. Again, the Holy Ghost felt it was needful to encourage the people to remember the words spoken before by the apostles of our Lord Jesus Christ. There needs to be a resurgence of the preaching of the words of the apostles of Christ! Regretfully you do not hear apostolic preaching in this hour anymore.

> There needs to be a resurgence of the preaching of the words of the apostles of Christ!

Jude 18

How that they told you there should be mockers in the last time, who should walk after their own ungodly lust.

Notice with me in verse 18, Jude is referencing the previous verse in how the apostles of our Lord Jesus Christ warned us that there would be mockers in the last days. This is why apostolic preaching is so important, although we hear very little apostolic preaching today. Rather than apostolic preaching, we are receiving lollipops and cotton candy, which again demonstrates the carnality within the church.

Some time ago, I had a dream. And in this dream, there was a powerful beam of light that was shining into the darkness and all I could see was a clown that looked like 'Bozo, the clown' literally. I sensed in my spirit that God was trying to show me how ministers are literally clowning around. Today my friend is not the time to be clowning. Rather we need apostolic, Holy Ghost, Spirit-filled preaching.

When certain men continue to operate among us and retain their ungodliness, they demonstrate openly that they are mockers. They mock us, because they are able to remain in our

presence without being reproved by the Holy Scriptures and
rebuked by godly leadership. Regretfully, church leadership
fails to rebuke those who are out of the way. Paul, the apostle,
declared in 1st Timothy 5:20-21,

> *Them that sin rebuked before all, that others also may fear.
> I charge thee before God, and the Lord Jesus Christ, and the
> elect angels, that thou observe these things without prefer-
> ring one before another, doing nothing by partiality.*

The old cliché is correct, "It is not what you know but who
you know!" There are many ministers whose sins should have
been dealt with, but they were shown partiality because of corrupt leadership. Those men who erred should have been sat
down and disciplined, but rather they were exalted and promoted. No one believes in for-
giveness and reconciliation any
more than I, but we have lost the
spirit of correction in the body of
Christ today. I preached a mes-

> Regretfully, church
> leadership fails to
> rebuke those who
> are out of the way.

sage some years ago entitled, *"Some needed correction within
the Church"* and I took my text from Jeremiah 7:28, *"But thou
shalt say unto them, this is a nation that obeyeth not the voice
of the Lord their God, nor receiveth correction: truth is perished,
and is cut off from their mouth."* I know a message with that
title today would not go too far or be received very well.

Most people feel they have no need for correction in this
church era. When leadership fails to take a stand against sin, it
will then leaven the whole lump. Paul said in Galatians 5:7-9,
*"Ye did run well; who did hinder you that ye should not obey
the truth? This persuasion cometh not of him that calleth you. A
little leaven leaventh the whole lump."*

Regretfully, we are in the shape we're in because we are

too concerned with being politically correct. God, the father, through the Holy Ghost, forewarned the churches that evil would seek a place of residence within the church but seemingly, no one cares. Every epistle is addressed to the church to correct error or negate sin that may find its way into the body. If the leadership does not arise and stand for godliness, then just as in the days of Eli, the lampstand will go out in the houses of God. The psalmist cried in Psalms 94:16, *"Who will rise up for me against the evil doers? Or who will stand up for me against the workers of iniquity?"*

Leadership is challenged to rise up and stand up against sin. But, because of political correctness, men are afraid to do so. True leadership is demanded to stand up, because leadership always brings clarity. Say what you will, many Pentecostal denominations are no longer fluid neither are they fervent in the Holy Ghost. Even the gifts of the Holy Ghost have all but waned in the realm of Pentecostalism. While the spirit has been waning, the love of many has been waxing cold and indifferent.

Jesus said in Matthew 24:12,*"And because iniquity shall abound, the love of many shall wax cold"*. Every true God-called Minister should labor untiringly to keep the church pure and freed from sin. But modernistic theology has negated old-fashioned Holy Ghost conviction, and that is why we are where we are today. As a Minister of the Gospel, I see a famine of God's word in our churches. I recognize that men spend more time seeking worldly pleasure rather than seeking the counsel of God Almighty.

Jesus made it clear in Matthew 6:21, *"For where your treasure is there will your heart be also."* There is far too much grandstanding within the pulpits and not enough prayer and fasting. Preachers have become politicians when they should be public criers instead. Prayer and fasting will humble a man's soul, drive him to greater hunger, and thirst for the righteousness of God.

I know for the most part my ministry is old school, but you will never know how many men and women write me, phone me or e-mail me and declare to me how God is setting them free from pornography, immorality, adultery, fornication, alcohol, and a plethora of other sins. Every day someone contacts me and testifies to some form of deliverance from bondage that was once in their lives. Therefore, I cannot become derelict in my calling while on guard. Grown men will call me and weep profusely trying to aggregate their emotions so they can tell me what great and powerful things God is doing within their lives. They plead with me relentlessly, please keep preaching it straight and do not even consider letting up.

Every man or woman called of God has been charged to preach the word of the Lord in season and out of season. That means, when they want to hear it and when they do not want to hear it. Regretfully, we are living in an hour when men do not want to hear the word of God. Everyone who claims to be a God-called Minister and fails to preach the word of God is committing spiritual treason. Every God-called Minister is under command by God to preach against sin, lest sin corrupt and destroy the church of the living God. The prophet Isaiah heralded in Isaiah 58:1, "*Cry aloud, spare not, lift up thy voice like a trumpet, and show my people their transgressions, and the house of Jacob their sins.*" Modern-day preachers are afraid to preach against sin and reprimand the people for their transgressions. Because we have become soft on sin, sin now has dominion and authority in most of our churches. Too many churches, today, are controlled by boards, but I say - take those boards outside, nail them on the wall and give place to the Holy Spirit and the word of God.

What harsh judgment will be upon those who proclaim they are God-called, but never cried aloud against the sins and transgressions of the parishioners. That is the very reason God gave gifts to men, so that they could preach against the sins that are in the church and keep the church in a posture of godliness. In the middle of the word *apostasy,* we see the word *"post"*. Once you leave your *post,* you will ultimately become an apostate. To every God-called minister I say unto you, remain steadfast at your post in spite of popularity. I had rather be popular with God and the Holy Ghost than to receive the accolades and praise of men. If you remain steadfast at your post, you will be mocked, for they mocked Christ our Lord. While hanging on the cross, Jesus was despised and openly shamed, yet he opened not his mouth.

> To every God-called minister I say unto you, remain steadfast at your post in spite of popularity.

Every day in America, we witness a mockery of the truth. From the White House to the halls of Congress, what is taking place is a grave travesty and mockery. As you listen to the sound bites of politicians and even the President of these United States, it is unfathomable, how blatantly they adamantly lie. Truly, these men have no fear of God Almighty. This ungodly mockery has found its way into the Church of the living God. Ministers have also fallen into the same snare and trap of the enemy. They openly lie without any Holy Ghost conviction as to what they say is knowingly wrong and sinful. Men, today, have lost their God consciousness and their minds have become seared with a hot iron. The Church has become a place of entertainment rather than a place for Holy Ghost edification and worship. Churches have become mere social clubs with social gatherings and for many they are looking for partnership rather than fellowship in the Holy Ghost. Do not misunderstand me. I found my spouse attending church even though I was not seeking a spouse, but rather I was seeking the Lord God of Abraham. My spouse was a blessing to me, because of my diligent seeking of the Lord Jesus Christ. I sought the Lord, and he added those to me, which I needed.

According to the Greek, a *mocker* is described as a *false teacher.* Thus, we read in here 2nd Peter 3:3,

> *Knowing this first, that there shall come in the last days scoffers, walking after their own lust, and saying, where is the promise of his coming? For since the fathers fell asleep all things continue as they were from the beginning of the creation.*

I want to remind you that what we are witnessing today are the same signs and prophecies that Jude gave concerning certain men, the fallen angels, the sodomites, and ungodly teachers. Make no mistake about it; the word of Almighty God is coming to fruition as I write this book.

In January of 2012, while, in a time of prayer and fasting, God dropped a word into my spirit, *acceleration.* After the presidential elections, the Lord said 'everything would begin to accelerate exponentially.' You are witnessing that acceleration at this very moment.

Jude 19

These be they who separate themselves, sensual, having not the spirit.

When Jude uses the pronoun *they,* he is referring to the certain men that 'crept in unawares' and separate themselves because they are sensual and have not the Holy Ghost. If we, as believers, reject as well as grieve the Holy Ghost, we too will become sensual. The fact that they are sensual simply means that they have returned to their beastly and carnal ways. Every man is a beast without the spirit of God. It is the Spirit of God abiding within a man, which makes the man spiritual and leads him to negate his carnal ways. Without God's presence in a person's life, they instinctively are reduced to a brute beast.

That is the very reason Jesus emphasized the baptism of the Holy Ghost prior to his ascension. Jesus knew how imperative it would be to walk in the Holy Ghost in these perilous days in which we are living. If we do not walk in the Holy Ghost, we too will be taken captive by Satan at his will. Remember, it was Satan that desired and demanded Peter's soul. But thank God, Jesus Christ prayed for Peter, that his faith fail not and when he was converted, he was told to strengthen the brethren.

Let me remind you, it is Satan's desire to bring you into captivity. Paul declared in 2nd Timothy 2:26, *"And that they may recover themselves out of the snare of the devil, who were taken captive by him at his will"*. The term *captive* means to be literally *taken alive*. It is Satan's motive to induce sin into a person's life while they are alive and hasten their death, so they die in a condition of broken fellowship with Christ our Lord. Once a believer dies and goes to be with the Lord, Satan can no longer attempt to invoke sin in their lives.

Jesus admonished Peter, after his conversion, to strengthen the brethren. I learned from that passage of Scripture that every Spirit-filled believer has the ability to strengthen one another by the Spirit of Christ that dwells within us. Therefore, it is my goal

> Every Spirit-filled believer has the ability to strengthen one another by the Spirit of Christ that dwells within us.

and desire to strengthen you as you read this book right now. I want to see you finish strong in the Lord and in the power of his might.

Jude said that these certain men separate themselves from the godly. I say, the godly should no doubt separate themselves from these certain men and false teachers. We are told in 2nd Corinthians 6:14, *"Be ye not on equally yoked together with unbelievers: for what fellowship hath righteousness with unrighteousness? And what communion hath light with darkness?"* We must understand that there will be a separation between the godly and the ungodly. To separate one's self is not to be arrogant or to esteem oneself more highly than another, but rather to keep ourselves unspotted from this present world.

The Lord will purge his floor, separate the chaff from the wheat at his seconding coming, and gather the wheat into his garner. Satan wants to stain everyone's wedding garment in order to not be found worthy to enter into the Marriage Supper of The Lamb. Looking back at verse 12, Jude said these entities are 'spots in your feast'. We are told in 2nd Timothy 3:5, *"Having a form of godliness, but denying the power thereof: from such turn away."* It is not bigotry or self-righteousness to turn away from the ungodly. We are told by Paul the apostle, "from such turn away" or get out of their midst. We had better become like the man of God Joseph and flee wickedness when we find it in close proximity to our doorstep.

That was Cain's problem. Sin was lying at his door. These certain men have already lost the anointing and Spirit of God from their lives. If you continue to intermingle with them, you too will lose your anointing; it is called usurpation. The anointing of the Holy Ghost is a sacred blessing and virtue my friend, thus never allow it to be ruined, tainted or usurped. Satan desires to usurp everyone's anointing, especially in these last days.

The people that Paul warned us of have a form of godliness, but there is no power of the Holy Ghost operating fluidly within their lives or ministries. Again, they are 'wells without water' and 'clouds without rain'.

There is nothing as great and refreshing as a fresh baptism in the Holy Ghost. Just like water on parched soil, it will revive the spirit and soul man.

Jude 20

But ye, beloved, building up yourselves on your most holy faith, praying in the Holy Ghost.

J esus Christ is the chief cornerstone and the foundation upon which the child of God builds their life. It is upon the foundation of the apostles and prophets in which we continue to build thereon. We read in Ephesians 2:19-22,

Now therefore ye are no more strangers and foreigners, but fellow citizens with the saints, and of the household of God; and are built upon the foundation of the apostles and prophets, Jesus Christ himself being the chief cornerstone; in whom all the building fitly framed together growth unto a holy temple in the Lord: in whom ye also are builded together for a habitation of God through the spirit.

Every child of God is a builder and must build upon Jesus Christ and the foundation of the apostles and prophets. We find this proof found in 1st Corinthians 2:10 -17,

According to the grace of God which is given unto me, as a wise master builder, I have laid the foundation, and another buildeth there on. But let every man take heed how he buildeth there upon. For other foundation can no man lay than that is laid, which is Jesus Christ. Now if any man build upon this foundation gold, silver, precious stones, wood,

*hays, stubble; Every man's work shall be made manifest: for
the day shall declare it, because it shall be revealed by fire;
and the fire shall try every man's work of what sort it is. If
any man's work abide which he hath build thereupon, he
shall receive a reward. If any man's work shall be burned, he
shall suffer loss: but he himself shall be saved; yet so as by
fire. Know ye not that ye are the temple of God, and that the
spirit of God dwelleth in you? If any man defile the temple of
God, him shall God destroyed; for the temple of God is holy,
which temple ye are.*

Of course, Jesus Christ is the master architect of redemption. However, Paul the apostle described himself as a master
builder. A master builder is a chief constructor or craftsman.
Paul was chosen to be such a one. As a child of God, if you
build upon hay, wood, or stubble you will be consumed by the
fire of Almighty God at his sec-
ond coming. However, what is
often overlooked in this passage
is that if we build upon gold, silver, and precious stones they too
will be tried by fire, but these are

> We must build solely
> and completely
> upon the word of
> God, which is Jesus
> Christ, the chief
> cornerstone.

certainly more durable. Nevertheless, Jesus is the chief cornerstone. Although gold, silver, and precious stones may not be
burned in the fire they can be melted by the intensity of the
heat. Therefore, we must build solely and completely upon the
word of God, which is Jesus Christ, the chief cornerstone.

Paul said that every man's work will be tried by fire, and
that is the fire of God. We must all be building right now for
there is a ferocious storm just over the horizon. If you build
on Christ Jesus, once the storm has passed you will remain
standing. If you build upon anything other than Christ, our
Lord, all will be lost. This is why it is important to remember

the words of the apostles of our Lord Jesus Christ, because it is upon his apostles and prophets that the foundation is partially built with Jesus Christ being the chief cornerstone.

Jude says we are to build up ourselves on our most holy faith. Faith can only be increased by the word of God. Notice Romans 10:17, *"So then faith cometh by hearing, and hearing by the word of God."* When we hear the word of God, which is Jesus Christ, then our faith will grow exponentially. It is required of us that our faith grows, or we cannot please God. According to the Scripture, the only thing that I know that has ever pleased God is faith. We read in Hebrews 11:6,

> But without faith it is impossible to please him: for he that cometh to God must believe that he is, and that he is a rewarder of them that diligently seek him.

Our building *(spiritual labor)* allows our building *(the body of Christ)* to grow as our faith grows: I hope you grasp what I just said. Remember, it was by faith that Noah built an ark for the saving of his house. It takes real faith to build anything, especially when it comes to the ministry.

As our faith grows through the building *(the process of labor through building)*, we, therefore, learn to pray in the Holy Ghost. Since the Holy Ghost is for the purpose of edification, which simply means to build up, then the Holy Ghost helps us build greater things for the glory of God. This is why it is imperative to be Spirit-filled, Spirit-led, and Spirit-controlled. It was the Spirit of God moving upon the face of the waters, which brought to fruition a new heaven and a new earth. When the Holy Ghost begins to move, he can move, or he can build anything we need. He can move mountains, and he can build kingdoms. Jude admonishes the believer to pray in the

Holy Ghost.

Paul the apostle declared in Romans 8:26,

Likewise the spirit also helpeth our infirmities: for we know not what we should pray for as we ought: but the spirit itself maketh intercession for us with groanings which cannot be uttered.

Never underestimate the power of the Holy Ghost, for he always knows how to pray. He is the one who helps us to pray and pray correctly. Paul, the apostle, also admonished us to pray in the Holy Ghost. Ephesians 6:18 says that we should be *"praying always with all prayer and supplication in the spirit"*. When one prays or supplicates in the Spirit, they are making profuse headway in every sense of the term. Jesus knew how great the need would be for the baptism in the Holy Ghost; thus, he prayed that we might receive the baptism in the Holy Ghost, just as he did.

Remember, Jesus never performed one miracle until he was baptized in the river of Jordan and the Holy Ghost descended upon him in the form of a dove. He was then led up of the Spirit into the wilderness to be tempted of the devil. Once he came back to Jerusalem, according to Luke chapter 4, he declared emphatically, "the Spirit of the Lord is upon me, because he hath anointed me." If Jesus needed to have the baptism in the Holy Ghost, do you think we need the baptism in the Holy Ghost?

Jesus said in John 14:16-17,

And I will pray the father, and he shall give you another comforter, that he may abide with you forever; even the spirit of truth; whom the world cannot receive, because it seeth him not, neither knoweth him: but ye know him; for he dwelleth with you, and shall be in you.

Before I move on, let me address one more issue. There are three distinct things that a believer and a nonbeliever can do concerning the Holy Ghost.

1. The first thing that both parties can do is resist the Holy Ghost. Stephen said in Acts 7:51, "*Ye stiff-necked and uncircumcised in heart and ears, ye do always resist the Holy Ghost: as your fathers did, so do ye.*" Let me encourage you never to resist the leadership of the Holy Ghost.

2. Second, both parties can grieve the Holy Ghost. We read in Ephesians 4:30, "*And grieve not the Holy Spirit of God, whereby ye are sealed unto the day of redemption*". As a believer, we are not to live an ungodly lifestyle wherein we make the Holy Ghost sorrowful for the way we are living and the way we are behaving. Every Spirit-filled believer is filled with grief, simultaneously, with the Holy Spirit, when they sin or transgress God. Both parties and are grieved with sorrow. We are one in the spirit and thus, when we sin we grieve the Holy Spirit. An unbeliever can also grieve the Holy Ghost by spurning his call to repentance.

3. Third, believers and nonbelievers can quench the Holy Ghost. Paul, the apostle, declared in 1st Thessalonians 5:19, "*Quench not the spirit.*" The term *quench* simply means *to put out the fire of God.* When the Spirit of God begins to move, instead of trying to put out his fervency and fiery disposition, we should allow the fire to burn brightly and deeply within our hearts. The fire of the Holy Ghost will radically burn out the sin in a person's life if allowed. The fire is what refines and burns out the dross. And of course, a nonbeliever can quench or put out the pleading of the Holy Ghost in trying to lead them to repentance.

I trust you understand the importance and significance of praying in the Holy Ghost. Do not be afraid to let the Holy

Ghost pervade your spirit and speak through you. Do not try to dictate the sounds or the words. You will hear the words from the Spirit of God in your spirit or your innermost being. You are the one to speak those words and let them come forth. A believer is just like a trumpet, a musician must put wind to the horn for it to make a sound. The believer is the horn, and the Holy Ghost is the wind and when you allow the wind to flow through you fluidly he will give you the utterance but you will make the sound. Receiving the baptism in the Holy Ghost is not difficult. However, it can be, if you quench him or do not yield yourself completely to him. Do not ever grow weary seeking God for a deeper experience in the Holy Ghost. He is a well of salvation to all men.

Jude 21

Keep yourselves in the love of God, looking for the mercy of our Lord Jesus Christ unto eternal life.

In closing his epistle, Jude admonishes the children of God to keep ourselves confined to the love of God. If you keep Jesus Christ in your heart, Jesus Christ will keep you. As I said earlier, men can grieve the Holy Ghost and men can also walk away from the Lord if they chose.

Jesus said in John 6:66-67, *"From that time many of his disciples went back, and walked no more with him. Then said Jesus unto the twelve, will ye also go away."* Again, it all boils down to a simple choice. How timely he made this statement in this chapter and verse - 6:66. Peter gives us a detailed understanding as to how the child of God will be kept in 1st Peter 1:5, *"Who are kept by the power of God through faith unto salvation ready to be revealed in the last time"*. First, Peter says we are kept by the power of God or the Holy Spirit. But we are only kept by the power of God as long as *we keep* our faith in him and the work that he wrought at Calvary.

Peter then shares an end time revelation about those who are kept by the power of God. Those God keeps will be re-

vealed or made manifest in the last days. These believers are
going to be the ones endued with power from on high to con-
front Satan and his minions. This faction or group of people
will be revealed or disclosed in the last days. The word *time* in
the Greek means *a divinely appointed time* when foreordained
events must come to pass. This word, *time,* is the same word
that Paul used to describe Christ birth as being in the fullness
of *time.* Both Christ birth and the revelation of those who are
kept by the power of God are at a divinely appointed time.

That is the reason Jesus admonished the disciples in Acts
1:8,

> *But ye shall receive power, after that the Holy Ghost is come
> upon you: and ye shall be witnesses unto me both in Jerusa-
> lem, and in all Judea, and in Samaria, and unto the utter-
> most part of the earth.*

The main purpose for the baptism in the Holy Ghost is to
receive power from God for his service. That is the very reason
the church is so anemic and im-
potent, because fewer and fewer
people are living and walking in
the power of the Holy Ghost. The
Holy Ghost has come to give us power so we might produce
lasting works as we serve Christ and others. Jesus said, 'For
without me, you can do nothing'.

> The main purpose for the baptism in the Holy Ghost is to receive power from God for his service.

There are so many people trying to do spiritual things in
the kingdom of God, but they do not have the power of God
for service. We are made to realize the importance of the Holy
Ghost in Zachariah 4:6, *"Not by might, nor by power, but by
my spirit saith the Lord of hosts."* It will not be by the power of
men that we will accomplish the works of God, but rather by

the power of the Holy Ghost. The word *kept* in verse 21 simply means *to guard against loss or injury.* God is going *to keep* his remnant by the power of God to be revealed in these last days.

Therefore, we must keep our eyes upon Jesus, for he is the epitome of love. The believer is to be steadfast, and we must also hold fast. Paul, the apostle, said in 1st Corinthians 15:57-58,

> *But thanks be to God, which giveth us the victory through our Lord Jesus Christ. Therefore, my beloved brethren, be ye steadfast, unmovable, always abounding in the work of the Lord, for as much as ye know that your labor is not in vain in the Lord.*

I want to emphasize the word therefore found in verse 58. The word *therefore* means, *as the results of God giving us the victory or power,* we must remain steadfast, unmovable, and always abounding in the work of the Lord. Every believer is to know that their work and labor are not in vain. When you walk in victory you know what you are doing will not be in vain. The child of God who does service for the Lord will not go unrewarded. Paul tells us in Hebrews 6:10,

> *For God is not unrighteous to forget your work and labor of love, which ye have showed toward his name, in that ye have ministered to the saints, and do minister.*

God Almighty will never forget what you do regarding his kingdom. Neither will he be a debtor to any man. He will always reward those who walk after him and work for him with a pure heart and clean hands.

Not only should we be steadfast, but we must hold fast. In Revelation 3:11-12,

> *Behold, I come quickly: hold that fast which thou hast, that no man take thy crown. Him that overcometh, will I make a*

pillar in the temple of my God, and he shall go no more out: and I will write upon him the name of my God.

Here Jesus said to let no man or person steal your crown. Those whom Jude speaks of are the ones stealing the crowns of many believers. Paul said in 1st Thessalonians 5:21, *"Prove all things; hold fast that which is good"*. It is imperative that every ministry be proven. We are to know them that labor among us, in other words. 'Try the spirit!' The reason for 'trying the spirit' is because, so many of the ungodly are in our midst. Truth never fails a spiritual examination, no matter what the cost or the test. Once something has been proven good and worthy of acceptance, then we must hold fast to it. That is why Jesus Christ remains the Captain of our salvation and the anchor of our soul. Because Jesus is our High Priest, we have something to which we can hold fast. We read in Hebrews 4:14, *"Seeing then that we have a great high priest, that is passed into the heavens, Jesus the Son of God, let us hold fast our profession."*

I want to encourage you to always hold fast to the truth, along with sound biblical doctrine. If a person truly keeps themselves in the love of God, they can expect the mercy of God to always be there. Thus, we read the words of Paul the apostle found here in Hebrews 13:5-6,

Let your conversation being without covetousness; and be content with such things as ye have: for he hath said, I will never leave thee, nor forsake thee. So that we may boldly say, the Lord is my helper, and I will not fear what man shall do unto me.

Be assured, if God is in your life, you will know his mercy, because, his goodness and mercy are an extension of his presence. We read in Psalms 147:11, *"The Lord taketh pleasure in them that fear him, in those that hope in his mercy"*. Every child of God is to hold fast to the mercy of God every day. Because of his extenuating mercy, we will not fall under his judgment. The psalmist declared in Psalms 103:10, *"He hath not dealt with us after our sins; nor rewarded us according to our iniquities"*. If God rewarded every man according to his sins and personal failures, none of us would ever have a chance. If there were no mercy, we would never be afforded an opportunity to be in his presence. However, 'in his presence is fullness of joy'.

The psalmist fully understood the degree of God's mercy found in Psalms 130:3-4, *"If thou, Lord, shouldest mark iniquities, O Lord, who shall stand? But there is forgiveness with thee, that thou mayest be feared."* If the Father stood before a chalkboard and put a mark down every time we sinned or erred in any way, who would be able to stand? 'There is none righteous, no not one.' But the psalmist declared, 'there is forgiveness with thee'. It is because of his love and mercy that there is always forgiveness.

I trust we all will be quick to repent, live at the foot of the cross, and remain humble in this hour. Jesus Christ never refuses a broken and contrite heart. Notice the words of Luke 1:50, *"And his mercy is on them that fear him from generation to generation"*. The way to get the mercy of God is to fear God and honor him. The reason this nation is on the precipice of judgment and will be without mercy is because as a nation, we no longer fear God and reverence him. There is a wholesome fear that must be embraced in the heart of everyone.

Solomon declared in Proverbs 1:7, *"The fear of the Lord is the beginning of knowledge: but fools despise wisdom and instruction."* The principle part of knowing God means to fear and honor him. Undoubtedly, few people today understand who God is. If it were not for the grace and mercy of God, many of you reading this book would have already been lost and would now be in eternity. I love Ephesians 2:4,

> But God, who is rich in mercy, for his great love wherewith he loved us, even when we were dead in sins, hath quickened us together with Christ, by grace are ye saved.

While many of us were still living in sin, God the Father, through his Son, Jesus Christ, commended his love toward us while we were yet sinners, all because he is rich in mercy. Mankind can never fathom nor grasp the riches of his mercy. Mountains of grace and oceans of mercy have been bestowed upon each of us.

Notice the words of Paul in Romans 9:15, *"For he saith to Moses, I will have mercy on whom I will have mercy, and I will have compassion on whom I will have compassion"*. Humankind does not realize the gravity of God's mercy shown to us repeatedly. Even with Israel being blind and obstinate towards the Lord Jesus Christ, he has promised to show them mercy as well, for we read in Romans 11:32, *"For God hath concluded them all in unbelief, that he might have mercy upon all."*

I would be dishonest if I said I fully understood this verse. However, I know one thing concerning the sovereignty of Almighty God. He says that he has 'concluded' all of Israel in unbelief, in order to have mercy upon them all; I believe that. Thank God, while I was estranged and away from God, he too had mercy upon me. I trust that you too will find the mercy and grace of God daily as you walk with him. Be assured there is more than enough mercy for us all. The psalmist David summed it up beautifully in Psalms 37:23-25,

> *The steps of a good man are ordered by the Lord: and he delighted in his way. Though he fall, he shall not be utterly cast down: for the Lord up holdeth him with his hand. I have been young, and now am old; yet have I not seen the righteous forsaken, nor his seed begging bread.*

Although a man stumble and fall, he is not utterly cast down because the mercy of the Lord will hold him up. I remember when my children were small I would hold them by their hands although they would stumble while walking across the parking lot I had the power to hold them up lest they fall and skin their knees. In my mind, that is a picture of God as he holds each of us in the palm of his hand.

Jude 22

And of some have compassion, making a difference.

Every believer is required to be compassionate when it comes to the lost. We are to have conviction concerning the lost and the backslider in regards to trying to bring them to the saving grace and knowledge of Christ our Lord.

Where would you be today without the compassion of Christ in your life? Mature Christians should be a light in this dark world among false teachers and false prophets. If men of God wield the truth, sinners will come to the light in spite of the darkness. Jesus said in John 3:21, *"But he that doeth truth cometh to the light, that his deeds may be manifest, that they are wrought in God"*. For most of my ministry, I have always prayed that God would give me great compassion towards the lost and allow me to preach with deep Holy Ghost conviction that would draw men to him.

We are to be the salt and the light in the earth. Jesus Christ is still the light of the world. Jesus said of himself in John 8:12, *"I am the light of the world: he that followeth me shall not walk in darkness, but shall have the light of life."* Needless to say, it is

truly up to the believers to make a difference in this convolut-
ed and sinful world.

The word *difference* here means *to separate thoroughly* or
to literally *withdraw thy self from others.* Again, true believers
cannot fellowship with those in darkness. The fact we are to
have compassion upon sinners does not mean we must lose
our convictions relative to sin. If we lose our conviction relative to sin, we will no longer make a difference in the world.
Only Christians can make a lasting difference in this present
world. Through the power of the Holy Ghost, the church is
supposed to be the salt and the light in the earth. The salt is
the agent that preserves the church and the light leads men to
redemption through the blood of Jesus Christ. I trust it is your
heart's desire to be Spirit-led. As a believer, we are the only
ones that can truly make a difference in this present world before the return of Christ. It is my desire that you strive daily to
live a godly life in this present world so to make a difference
that will last for all eternity.

Jude 23

And others save with fear, pulling them out of the fire; hating even the garment spotted by the flesh.

J ude says that we must save others with fear. Why? The reason we must save others with fear is because, in the last days, there will be a great waning when it comes to the fear of the Lord.

It is evident, as the Lord tarries, many of these certain men and false prophets will believe they are justified in their ungodly deeds. They must be dealt with because they will be eternally lost if their error is not challenged by spiritual authority and leadership. Paul, the apostle, declared in Romans 3:18, *"There is no fear of God before their eyes."* Every day in this nation, there seems to be a greater loss of fear and reverence toward the things of God. The more callused and hardhearted men become the less fear they evidence towards God.

There was a time when all men had a certain degree of fear and were afraid to do certain things or live a certain way because of a godly fear. The indifference of mankind has become literally unbelievable in this hour. The heart of man is seemingly fixed towards doing evil continually. Solomon, a man of profound wisdom, made a very disturbing statement and prophecy in Ecclesiastes 8:11, *"Because sentence against an evil work is not executed speedily, therefore the heart of the sons of men is fully set in them to do evil."* This verse clearly demonstrates that due to the mercy of God and because God does not execute judgment speedily; men will sin and commit evil in even greater and more detrimental ways. Notice the next verse, Ecclesiastes 8:12, *"Though a sinner do evil a hundred times, and his days be prolonged, yet surely I know that it shall be well with them that fear God, which fear before him."* Simply put, it is only by the fear of God that men depart from evil.

Jude was emphasizing that a definite reverence and fear of God Almighty would be needed to endure the last days. What I find very disturbing is that Jude said spiritually, these false teachers are already in the fire of hell and are not aware of it. Though these souls are not presently in hell; that is their ultimate doom

> A definite reverence and fear of God Almighty would be needed to endure the last days.

and destiny unless we pull them from the fire, and they repent. Therefore, Jude said, "save with fear, pulling them from the fire". Pulling them from the fire is to siege them by force. Jesus said in Matthew 11:12, *"And from the days of John the Baptist until now, the kingdom of heaven suffereth violence, and the violent take it by force."*

They are destined to the fire of hell because they are lost. They do not realize that their wedding garment is spotted by the flesh. Because they are doomed in the fire, the child of God is compelled to move with conviction and pull them out of harm's way if possible and that by force. Everyone's wedding garment must be holy, white raiment. The master of the house, who is King of the Marriage Supper of The Lamb, will not allow anyone to come into the feast with a spotted garment.

Paul said in Ephesians 5:27, "*That he might present it to himself a glorious church, not having spot, or wrinkle, or any such thing; but that it should be holy and without blemish.*" Let us take a close look at the parable of the wedding banquet Jesus gave in Matthew 22:11-14,

> *And when the King came in to see the guest, he saw there was a man which had not on a wedding garment: and he said unto him friend (in a negative connotation), how camest thou in hither not having a wedding garment? And he was speechless. Then said the king to the servants, bind him hand and foot, and take him away, and cast him into outer darkness; there shall be weeping and gnashing of teeth. For many are called, but few are chosen.*

This man came stealthy into the wedding feast without the proper wedding garment. This parable clearly describes the evil of self-righteousness and carnal works. Jesus Christ is the one who returned to heaven to prepare every one of us a wedding garment for the wedding banquet. Jesus did not return to heaven to literally build us a mansion of sorts next door to himself or the Father. Jesus went to build and design us a wedding garment that will ultimately cloth us and allow us to enter into the marriage banquet.

Many have misunderstood the words of Christ found in John 14:1-3,

> *Let not your heart be troubled: ye believe in God, believe also in me. In my father's house are many mansions (a place of abode i.e. residence): if it were not so, I would have told you. I go to prepare a place for you. And if I go and prepare a place for you, I will come again, and receive you unto my-*

self; that where I am, there ye may be also.

I want to try to explain to you in my own clumsy way what Jesus went to build for us when he returned to heaven. He did not go to build you a mansion, but rather to prepare you a wedding garment. We find this profound revelation in 2nd Corinthians 5:1-4,

> For we know that if our earthly house of this tabernacle were dissolved, we have a building (dwelling place figuratively) of God, a house (a residence) not made with hands, eternal in the heavens. For in this we groan, earnestly desiring to be clothed upon with our house which is from heaven: if so be that being clothed we shall not be found naked. For we that are in this tabernacle do groan being burdened: not for that we would be unclothed, but clothed (superimposed, to place over or to cover) upon, that mortality might be swallowed up of life.

So, the *place* of residence that Jesus Christ has gone to prepare is actually a wedding garment. This wedding garment is so that we might be clothed in his righteousness *(to be superimposed over the child of God)* so that we might enter into the wedding banquet.

Some time ago God gave me a revelation that whatever sin, sickness, disease or anomaly that *sinners* die with, they will retain throughout all eternity. They will also be naked for all eternity, because they will never receive a new body like the redeemed, nor will they be clothed forever, because he did not prepare them a wedding garment. The sheer thought of that revelation should cause every man to desire to live a righteous and godly life. When one is naked, they feel tremendously vulnerable. Imagine feeling vulnerable throughout all eternity. Nakedness in itself will be eternal torment. It must be understood; God will not take his church *out* and *then make it glorious,* but he will make the church glorious *before he takes it out.* God, the Father, is going to present to his Son a glorious church, without spot, wrinkle or blemish.

That is why the church will go through the great tribulation to be perfected and made holy for the presentation to the Son. The church, however, is not appointed unto God's wrath, and that is scripturally clear in the word of God. We read in 1st Thessalonians 5:9-10, *"For God hath not appointed us to wrath, but to obtain salvation by our Lord Jesus Christ, who died for us, that, whether we wake or sleep, we should live together with him."* It is because of the blood of a lamb that the child of God is not appointed unto the wrath of God. Paul declared emphatically in Romans 5:9, *"Much more then, being now justified by his blood, we shall be saved from wrath through him".*

Jesus admonished the church, his body, to be clothed with the proper wedding garments. Notice the words of Christ directed to his church in Revelation 3:18,

> *I counsel thee to buy of me gold tried in the fire, that thou mayest be rich; and white raiment, that thou mayest be clothed, and that the shame of thy nakedness do not appear; and anoint thine eyes with eye salve, that thou mayest see.*

Here again, Jesus says that the wedding garment must be white raiment. Jesus also said that it would be a tremendous shame to be naked and to be exposed. This is why he has gone to prepare this beautiful wedding garment for every child of God. Jesus wants every blood bought born again child of God to not only be redeemed, but to be clothed in his righteousness white raiment. We are admonished in Revelation 16:15, *"Behold, I come as a thief, blessed is he that watcheth, and keepeth his garments, lest he walk naked, and they see his shame."* In this passage, Jesus tells us that we must keep our garment spotless. If you do your part, I assure you Christ will do his part.

We are admonished by John, that Jesus Christ will come as a thief and we must watch and keep our garment spotless lest we walk naked. If the wedding garment is soiled or sullied, we cannot enter in. The only thing that can keep the wedding garment spotless is the blood of the Lamb, the Word of God, and the power of the Holy Ghost. Paul declared in Ephesians 5:26, *"That he might sanctify and cleanse it with the washing of water by the word."* Paul says that the word of God will wash the child of God and keep us sanctified so that we may enter into the Marriage Supper of The Lamb.

We also read in Titus 3:5, *"Not by works of righteousness which we have done, but according to his mercy he saved us, by the washing of regeneration, and renewing of the Holy Ghost"*. It is the washing process of regeneration that keeps the believer cleansed and the renewing of the Holy Ghost that keeps us spotless.

As a believer, we all must hate and deplore sin of any kind. Hatred against sin and ungodliness will help keep the believer cleansed. We are admonished in Proverbs 8:13, *"The fear of the Lord is to hate evil: pride and arrogancy, and the evil way, and the froward mouth, do I hate."* It is evident, when one has the proper fear towards God; they will hate the works of the flesh that corrupt the soul. It still remains 'a fearful thing to fall into the hands of the living God'.

> As a believer, we all must hate and deplore sin of any kind.

I trust that you will always retain a godly fear within your heart. Paul declared emphatically in Hebrews 10:31, *"It is a fearful thing to fall into the hands of the living God".* May you remain fearful of him in these waning days?

Jude 24

Now unto him that is able to keep you from falling, and to present you faultless before the presence of his glory with exceeding joy.

Only God Almighty, through his sovereignty, can keep a man! Only the work of Christ at the cross can keep a man from falling. It is the nature of man to fall, but it is the power of Christ to keep him from falling. There are no works of righteousness that can preserve a man whatsoever. Man's righteousness is sadly deplorable and despicable, if I must say. We are admonished in Isaiah 64:6, *"But we are all as an unclean thing, and all our righteousnesses are as filthy rags; and we all do fade as a leaf; and our iniquities, like the wind, have taken us away. "*

Man's religion and righteousness is a stench in the nostrils of God. Everything that man would dare bring to God is polluted and corrupted, through his fallen nature. The truth is, we are all an unclean subject before the Lord of Glory. If we try to stand in our own righteousness, he said we would be revealed as *filthy*. The word *filthy* in Hebrew speaks of the *menstrual flux* and the rags that were used by women during their monthly cycle. I am not trying to be crudely graphic here, only to explain how vile men are, when they try to present their own self-righteousness before God Almighty.

There is no man that can stand righteous before God, no matter how much he tries. The Bible is clear. Paul declared in Romans 3: 10, *"As it is written, there is none righteous, no, not one"*. God's righteousness is very simple, because when the father sees the blood applied to the heart of the believer, judgment will pass over them. Jehovah told Moses, "When I see the blood I will pass over you." The Lord even shed innocent blood to make coats of skin to cover Adam and Eve due to their nakedness and shame. Their self-righteousness drove them to sew fig leaves to cover themselves. Their self-righteousness, however, as with all men, is vain and worthless. Adam's effort was a frail attempt to cover his sin and nakedness. The only righteousness that a man will ever have is from the work of Christ accomplished at Calvary. Paul said in 2nd Corinthians 5:21, *"For he hath made him to be sin for us, who knew no sin; that we might be made the righteousness of God in him."* Because of the righteousness of Jesus Christ now imparted unto man, he now becomes a new creature and all things have passed away and behold all things are become new.

Because a man has been washed in the blood and redeemed by the spirit of God, we can now be presented to the father through Jesus Christ and be presented blameless.

That could never happen through self-righteousness no matter how hard one might try. Because a man has been washed in the blood and redeemed by the spirit of God, we can now be presented to the father through Jesus Christ and be presented blameless. That is truly hard to fathom and grasp, yet Paul declared in 1st Thessalonians 5:23,

And the very God of peace sanctify you wholly; and I pray God your whole spirit and soul and body be preserved blameless unto the coming of our Lord Jesus Christ.

Only by the blood of Jesus Christ can a man be presented to the father blameless. This is why Jude declares that only Christ is able to keep one from falling. The fact that he is able to keep a man from falling proves he is the only Savior of mankind. The fact he is able to keep us from falling proves his deity and majesty. Only Christ can present a man blameless, and he will do so with exceeding joy. We will partake of his glory and that partaking will be with exceeding joy at the second coming of Jesus Christ. We know that truth by the words of Peter the apostle found in 1st Peter 4:12-13,

Beloved, think it not strange (or foreign) concerning the fiery trial which is to try you, as though some strange thing happened unto you: but rejoice, inasmuch as ye are partakers of Christ sufferings; that, when his glory shall be revealed, ye may be glad also with exceeding joy.

Every blood-bought, born again child of God will partake and experience the same glory that Jesus possess at his second coming and on that resurrection day. To partake of that glory means to be clothed with immortality. This corruption must put on incorruption, and this mortal must put on immortality.

I look forward to the day when I shall receive my new wedding garment: how about you?

Jude 25

To the only wise God our Savior, be glory and majesty, Dominion and power, both now and ever. Amen.

Jesus Christ personifies wisdom, and he knows what is best for each of us on a daily basis. The fact that he is the only wise God is all the more reason to trust him.

David declared in Psalms 68:19, *"Blessed be the Lord, who daily loadeth us with benefits, even the God of our salvation"*. He is not only the God of our salvation, but every day he takes the time to load us with his benefits.

Paul said that the foolishness of God is wiser than men. How vast is his wisdom? Many times you may find yourself in a difficult place, however, do not become discouraged at your circumstances or situation. The reason is declared by Paul in Romans 8:18, *"For I reckon that the sufferings of this present time are not worthy to be compared with the glory which shall be revealed in us"*.

As a child of God, you must place your circumstances in the balances or scales of God. Once you weigh your sufferings, versus the glory that shall be revealed in you, it will be obvious that your suffering is not worthy to be compared to the glory that shall be revealed in you.

In closing, look with me please at Genesis 42:36, *"And Jacob their father said unto them, me have you bereaved of my children: Joseph is not, and Simeon is not, and ye will take Benjamin away: all these things are against me."* This truth is very simple. Everything that was happening in Jacob's life was for his good and not evil. However, from Jacob's natural disposition, he could not see how God, for many years, had been divinely working on his behalf, unknowingly. From Jacob's perception, he was living a life of bereavement; thinking Joseph was dead, and now Simeon was gone. Simeon was in prison in Egypt, and he said, "You will now take Benjamin away." Jacob was overwhelmed and felt everything was against him. The truth was, everything was working together for his own good.

Remember, perception is not always reality; it was not for Jacob and neither for you. How many times have we thought and believed one thing and then God proved he was doing some greater thing within our lives? Some of you reading this book feel like everything right now is against you. However, what you cannot see is that God is working to bring you into a better place.

> How many times have we thought and believed one thing and then God proved he was doing some greater thing within our lives?

May you be patient and trust God for what you cannot yet see. Jacob was not aware that God had sent Joseph before him to prepare a better life for him before he passed away. God is also preparing something better for you right now though you cannot see it. Paul declared in 1st Corinthians 2:9,

But as it is written, eye hath not seen, nor ear heard, neither

*have entered into the heart of man, the things which God
has prepared for them that love him. But God hath revealed
them unto us by his spirit: for the spirit search of all things,
yea, the deep things of God.*

Jacob had not seen, neither heard, nor had it entered into
his heart what God was doing for him. As a child of God, we
all become pessimistic at times, but I trust the Holy Ghost will
turn your pessimism into optimism.

What a profound statement Jude made when he declared
that Christ our Lord is the only wise God and Savior. May you
fully embrace this closing word from Jude and hide it in your
heart. I love this passage of Scripture in Jeremiah 10:6-7, *"Forasmuch as there is none like unto the, O Lord; thou art great,
and thy name is great in might. Who would not fear thee O King
of nations?"*

I pray that each of us retains a godly fear and reverence,
for there is truly no one like Jesus, the Lord's Christ. Will you
choose to fear the King of glory today? The race is not to the
swiftest nor to those who entered first, but to those who endure and finish the race, which the Lord has set before us all.